THE JESUS YOU MAY NOT KNOW

Study Guide

D1260278

DAVID JEREMIAH

with Dr. David Jeremiah

© 2020 Turning Point for God
P.O. Box 3838
San Diego, CA 92163
ALL RIGHTS RESERVED

Edited by Robert J. Morgan
Unless otherwise indicated, Scripture verses quoted are from the NEW KING JAMES VERSION.

All websites listed herein are accurate at the time of publication but may change in the future or cease to exist. The listing of website references does not imply endorsement of the site's entire contents.

Printed in the United States of America.

CONTENTS

ABOUT
DR. DAVID JEREMIAH
AND TURNING POINT

D r. David Jeremiah is the founder of Turning Point, a ministry committed to providing Christians with sound Bible teaching relevant to today's changing times through radio and television broadcasts, audio series, books, and live events. Dr. Jeremiah's common-sense teaching on topics such as family, prayer, worship, angels, and biblical prophecy forms the foundation of Turning Point.

David and his wife, Donna, reside in El Cajon, California, where he serves as the senior pastor of Shadow Mountain Community Church. David and Donna have four children and twelve grandchildren.

In 1982, Dr. Jeremiah brought the same solid teaching to San Diego television that he shares weekly with his congregation. Shortly thereafter, Turning Point expanded its ministry to radio. Dr. Jeremiah's inspiring messages can now be heard worldwide on radio, television, and the Internet.

Because Dr. Jeremiah desires to know his listening audience, he travels nationwide holding ministry events that touch the hearts and lives of many people. According to Dr. Jeremiah, "At some point in time, everyone reaches a turning point; and for every person, that moment is unique, an experience to hold onto forever. There's so much changing in today's world that sometimes it's difficult to choose the right path. Turning Point offers people an understanding of God's Word as well as the opportunity to make a difference in their lives."

Dr. Jeremiah has authored numerous books, including *Escape the Coming Night* (Revelation), *The Handwriting on the Wall* (Daniel), *Overcoming Loneliness, God in You* (Holy Spirit), *When Your World Falls Apart, 31 Days to Happiness—Searching for Heaven on Earth, Captured by Grace, What in the World Is Going On?, I Never Thought I'd See the Day!, Agents of the Apocalypse, RESET—Ten Steps to Spiritual Renewal, Signs of Life, Ten Questions Christians Are Asking, A Life Beyond Amazing, Perhaps Today, Overcomer, The Book of Signs, Everything You Need, Answers to Questions About Living in the Last Days,* and *Daily in His Presence.*

How to Use This Study Guide

The purpose of this Turning Point study guide is to reinforce Dr. David Jeremiah's dynamic, in-depth teaching and to aid the reader in applying biblical truth to his or her daily life. This study guide is designed to be used in conjunction with Dr. Jeremiah's *The Jesus You May Not Know* audio series, but it may also be used by itself for personal or group study.

Structure of the Lessons

Each lesson is based on one of the messages in the *The Jesus You May Not Know* compact disc series and focuses on specific passages in the Bible. Each lesson is composed of the following elements:

- *Outline*

The outline at the beginning of the lesson gives a clear, concise picture of the topic being studied and provides a helpful framework for readers as they listen to Dr. Jeremiah's teaching.

- *Overview*

The overview summarizes Dr. Jeremiah's teaching on the passage being studied in the lesson. Readers should refer to the Scripture passages in their own Bibles as they study the overview. Unless otherwise indicated, Scripture verses quoted are taken from the New King James Version.

- *Personal and Group Application Questions*

This section contains a variety of questions designed to help readers dig deeper into the lesson and the Scriptures, and to apply the lesson to their daily lives. For Bible study groups or Sunday school classes, these questions will provide a springboard for group discussion and interaction.

- *Did You Know?*

This section presents a fascinating fact, historical note, or insight that adds a point of interest to the preceding lesson.

PERSONAL STUDY

Thank you for selecting *The Jesus You May Not Know* for your current study. The lessons in this study guide were created to help you gain fresh insights into God's Word and develop new perspectives on topics you may have previously studied. Each lesson is designed to challenge your thinking and help you grow in your knowledge of Christ. During your study, it is our prayer that you will discover how biblical truth affects every aspect of your life and your relationship with Christ will be strengthened.

When you commit to completing this study guide, try to set apart a time, daily or weekly, to read through the lessons without distraction. Have your Bible nearby when you read the study guide, so you're ready to look up verses if you need to. If you want to use a notebook to write down your thoughts, be sure to have that handy as well. Take your time to think through and answer the questions. If you plan on reading the study guide with a small group, be sure to read ahead and be prepared to take part in the weekly discussions.

LEADER'S GUIDE

Thank you for your commitment to lead a group through *The Jesus You May Not Know*. Being a leader has its own rewards. You may discover that your walk with the Lord deepens through this experience. Throughout the study guide, your group will explore new topics and review study questions that encourage thought-provoking group discussion.

The lessons in this study guide are suitable for Sunday school classes, small-group studies, elective Bible studies, or home Bible study groups. Each lesson is structured to provoke thought and help you grow in your knowledge and understanding of God. There are multiple components in this section that can help you structure your lessons and discussion time, so make sure you read and consider each one.

Before You Begin

Before you begin each meeting, make sure you and your group are well-versed with the content of the chapter. Every person should have his or her own study guide so they can follow along and write in the study guide if need be. When possible, the study guide should be used with the corresponding compact disc series. You may wish to assign the study guide lesson as homework prior to the meeting of the group and then use the meeting time to listen to the CD and discuss the lesson.

To ensure that everyone has a chance to participate in the discussion, the ideal size for a group is around eight to ten people. If there are more than ten people, try to break up the bigger group into smaller subgroups. Make sure the members are committed to participating each week, as this will help create stability and help you better prepare the structure of the meeting.

At the beginning of the study each week, start the session with a question to challenge group members to think about the issues you will be discussing. The members can answer briefly, but the goal is to have an idea in their mind as you go over the lesson. This allows the group members to become engaged and ready to interact with the group.

After reviewing the lesson, try to initiate a free-flowing discussion. Invite group members to bring questions and insights they may have discovered to the next meeting, especially if they were unsure of the meaning of some parts of the lesson. Be prepared to discuss how biblical truth applies to the world we live in today.

Weekly Preparation

As the group leader, here are a few things you can do to prepare for each meeting:

- Choose whether or not you will play the CD message during your small group session.

  If you decide to play the CD message from Dr. Jeremiah as part of the meeting, you will need to adjust the group time accordingly.

- Make sure you are thoroughly familiar with the material in the lesson.

  Make sure you understand the content of the lesson so you know how to structure group time and you are prepared to lead group discussion.

- Decide, ahead of time, which questions you plan to discuss.

  Depending on how much time you have each week, you may not be able to reflect on every question. Select specific questions which you feel will evoke the best discussion.

- Take prayer requests.

  At the end of your discussion, take prayer requests from your group members and pray for each other.

Structuring the Discussion Time

If you need help in organizing your time when planning your group Bible study, here are two schedules, for sixty minutes and ninety minutes, which can give you a structure for the lesson:

Option 1 (Listen to Audio CD)	60 Minutes	90 Minutes
Welcome: Members arrive and get settled.	N/A	5 minutes
Getting Started Question: Prepares the group for interacting with one another.	Welcome and Getting Started 5 minutes	15 minutes
Message: Listen to the audio CD.	40 minutes	40 minutes
Discussion: Discuss group study questions.	10 minutes	25 minutes
Prayer and Application: Final application for the week and prayer before dismissal.	5 minutes	5 minutes

Option 2 (No Audio CD)	60 Minutes	90 Minutes
Welcome: Members arrive and get settled.	5 minutes	10 minutes
Getting Started Question: Prepares the group for interacting with one another.	10 minutes	10 minutes
Message: Review the lesson.	15 minutes	25 minutes
Discussion: Discuss group study questions.	25 minutes	35 minutes
Prayer and Application: Final application for the week and prayer before dismissal.	5 minutes	10 minutes

As the group leader, it is up to you to keep track of the time and keep things moving along according to your schedule. If your group is having a good discussion, don't feel the need to stop and move on to the next question. Remember, the purpose is to pull together ideas and share unique insights on the lesson. Make time each week to discuss how to apply these truths to living for Christ today.

The purpose of discussion is for everyone to participate, but don't be concerned if certain group members are more quiet—they may be internally reflecting on the questions and need time to process their ideas before they can share them.

Group Dynamics

Leading a group study can be a rewarding experience for you and your group members—but that doesn't mean there won't be challenges. Certain members may feel uncomfortable discussing topics that they consider very personal and might be afraid of being called on. Some members might have disagreements on specific issues. To help prevent these scenarios, consider the following ground rules:

- If someone has a question that may seem off topic, suggest that it is discussed at another time, or ask the group if they are okay with addressing that topic.

- If someone asks a question you don't know the answer to, confess that you don't know and move on. If you feel comfortable, invite other group members to give their opinions or share their comments based on personal experience.

- If you feel like a couple of people are talking much more than others, direct questions to people who may not have shared yet. You could even ask the more dominating members to help draw out the quiet ones.

- When there is a disagreement, encourage the group members to process the matter in love. Invite members from opposing sides to evaluate their opinions and consider the ideas of the other members. Lead the group through Scripture that addresses the topic, and look for common ground.

When issues arise, remind your group to think of Scripture: "Love one another" (John 13:34), "If it is possible, as much as depends on you, live peaceably with all men" (Romans 12:18), and "Be quick to listen, slow to speak and slow to become angry" (James 1:19, NIV).

FOR CONTINUING STUDY

For a complete listing of Dr. Jeremiah's materials for personal and group study call 1-800-947-1993, go online to www.DavidJeremiah.org, or write to Turning Point, P.O. Box 3838, San Diego, CA 92163.

Dr. Jeremiah's *Turning Point* program is currently heard or viewed around the world on radio, television, and the Internet in English. *Momento Decisivo*, the Spanish translation of Dr. Jeremiah's messages, can be heard on radio in every Spanish speaking country in the world. The television broadcast is also broadcast by satellite throughout the Middle East with Arabic subtitles.

Contact Turning Point for radio and television program times and stations in your area, or visit our website at www.DavidJeremiah.org/stationlocator.

THE JESUS YOU MAY NOT KNOW

INTRODUCTION

In his essay about Christ, "One Solitary Life," James Allen Francis wrote: "[Twenty] wide centuries have come and gone and today He is the centerpiece of the human race and the leader of the column of progress. I am far within the mark when I say that all the armies that ever marched, and all the navies that ever were built, and all the parliaments that ever sat, and all the kings that ever reigned, put together have not affected the life of man upon this earth as powerfully as has that One Solitary Life."

Jesus is more than just a familiar name. He was a real man who lived in human history, and there is no doubt about it. No reliable secular historian denies it. His life is recorded for us in the Bible, and we can learn much about Him. Because He rose from the grave and is alive, we can have a personal relationship with Him. Because He loves us, we can interact with Him, pray to Him, and have fellowship with Him.

The goal of this study is to become closer to Jesus. He is worth all the effort and time required. Philippians 3:8 says, "Yes, everything else is worthless when compared with the infinite value of knowing Christ Jesus my Lord" (NLT).

To love and know Christ is the first great goal of life, and the second is to make Him known to others. That's why we open our Bible to discover who He is and what He did, and that's why we open our mouth to praise and proclaim Him.

Because Jesus, being God, is infinite, we can always learn more about Him. None of us know Him as fully as we should, for Jesus is the mystery of the ages—the Almighty God whose throne is in heaven; the Nazarene Carpenter who wiped sweat from His brow; the Stranger of Galilee who napped in a boat; the Teacher whose wisdom changed the ethics of the world; the Prisoner whose crucifixion was excruciating; the Savior who bled for the world; the Corpse who borrowed a tomb; the Body who returned to life; the Hero who divided history into B.C. and A.D.; and the glorious King whose return is right on schedule.

So multifaceted is He that the Bible overflows with names, titles, and designations to describe Him. He is Jesus, the Nazarene, the Carpenter, the Rabbi. He is Immanuel—God with us; the Seed of Woman; the Dayspring from on high; the Consolation of Israel; the Messiah—Christ; the Prince of Peace and the King of Righteousness; the King of the Jews and the King of kings.

He is called the Lord, the Righteous Judge, the Good Shepherd, the Son of Abraham, the Son of David, the Son of Mary, the Son of Man, the Son of God. He is the Rock, the Living Stone, the Precious Cornerstone; and He's the foundation for life. He's the Lion of the Tribe of Judah, the Alpha and Omega, the First and the Last, the Redeemer, the Great High Priest, the Great Physician, the Lamb, the Man of Sorrows, the Lord whose Name is above every name.

How do you explain Someone like that?

However you're feeling, you'll be encouraged as you come to know Him more clearly and more deeply. Whatever your circumstances, they'll always be improved with Christ. Whatever your mood, it will be lifted as you see Him as He truly is.

In this series of lessons, we'll study various aspects of the personality, passion, and perfect work of Jesus Christ. In the process, may we discover afresh that everything else is worthless when compared with the infinite value of knowing Christ Jesus our Lord.

IS HE FROM HISTORY OR FROM ETERNITY?

Selected Scriptures

In this lesson we learn that Jesus loved us from eternity past, has placed eternity in our heart, and provides eternal life for us starting the moment we receive Him as Savior.

OUTLINE

We live in a transitory world in which, given enough time, everything will crumble and return to dust. Yet here we are, created with remarkable bodies—fearfully and wonderfully made—on a spinning planet perfectly suited to our needs. How do you make sense of it? If there's no God, life is absurd. But everything fits together perfectly through the reality that Jesus is the Everlasting Lord. He dwelt in the eternal past, has placed His eternal life in the hearts of His followers, and is preparing an eternal home for us. He is the Eternal Creator and Savior.

I. **Eternity in History: Jesus Loves Us**

II. **Eternity in Our Heart: Jesus Longs for Us**
   A. The Desire for Eternal Life
   B. The Description of Eternal Life

III. **Eternity in Heaven: Jesus Lives for Us**
   A. Jesus Is Providing for Us
   B. Jesus Is Praying for Us
   C. Jesus Is Protecting Us
   D. Jesus Is Preparing a Place for Us

Christ came into the world to be the instrument to provide eternal life for us all. His purpose in being here was to place eternal life within the reach of all mankind, to seek and to save. When He hung on the cross and cried, "It is finished," He was talking about the work necessary to provide eternal life for us.

Because of our sin and failures, our fellowship with the all-holy God was severed, but our all-holy God is also all-loving. The eternal God the Son came down to earth through the miracle of the virgin birth, lived a perfect life, and offered Himself as a sacrifice for our sins. His shed blood provided atonement, and His resurrection provided guaranteed hope for all who will come to God through Him. His death and resurrection guarantees eternal life for those who trust in Him.

Only an *eternal* God can bestow *eternal* life. What do we mean by eternal life? Some people envision it as simply an extension of this life into the future. But the Bible teaches there are two different destinations at the end of life. Those who deny Christ will spend eternity outside of God's fellowship; they are going to be alive forever somewhere, and the Bible uses terms like *hell* to describe it. The eternal life Jesus promised is not simply living forever. It is living forever in fellowship with God and His children in a place He has provided—and this eternal life doesn't begin when we die. It begins the moment we trust Jesus as our Savior.

ETERNITY IN HISTORY: JESUS LOVES US

Eternity is one of the great mysteries of God. It is the attribute of infinity in relation to time. It means that God has always existed. God the Father and His Son Jesus Christ live in the eternal present. If Jesus has always existed, that means that you too have been loved before the beginning of time. Ephesians 1:4 says, "He chose us in Him before the foundation of the world." God has loved you longer than you realize, for Jeremiah 31:3 says, "Yes, I have loved you with an everlasting love."

But nothing in this physical world is eternal. The words *eternity* and *eternal* are in a lot of movie and book titles, music albums, and song lyrics. *Eternity* is the name of a perfume, a mobile phone, a puzzle game, a superhero, a magazine, a newspaper, and a science fiction periodical. How ironic that a word meaning "forever" has been given as a name for many things that don't last very long!

We think of eternity as the extension of time, but eternity is not time. Eternity is beyond time. We don't understand eternity because we have no precedent. Life is ultimately meaningless and absurd if there's nothing beyond time. If we don't understand the reassurances God has given us in His Word, it's difficult to make it all the way through life. It's possible for us to discover the meaning of eternity only through the Person and the teachings of Jesus Christ and the Word of God.

Let's explore that meaning in three areas of life—eternity in history, eternity in our heart, and eternity in heaven. Eternity is one of the great mysteries of the universe, and it's one of the great mysteries of God. Eternity is the attribute of infinity in relationship to time. It means that the triune God—Father, Son, and Holy Spirit —has always existed. The past, present, and future as we know it are eternally present in the mind of God. God the Father and His Son Jesus Christ live in the eternal present.

We see life through three different lenses. We look backward into the past, we live in the fleeting present, and we make plans for the future. But when God looks at life, He doesn't see things that way. He sees everything in the eternal *now*. Everything is now to God. Everything is now to the Lord Jesus Christ. This is a mystery. It's difficult to get our mind around it, which is as it should be. If the God you worship is small enough for you to understand, He's not big enough for you to worship.

We can't understand all of this. Even when we've learned all we can learn about God, there's so much more about God we cannot know, for He is infinite and limitless. But we can know this: Jesus is God, and therefore He has no beginning and no end. He existed for endless ages before coming into the world to be our Savior. The Old Testament prophet Micah, for example, said of the Messiah's birth in Bethlehem, "Yet out of you [Bethlehem] shall come forth to Me the One to be Ruler in Israel, whose goings forth are from of old, from everlasting" (Micah 5:2).

Jesus Himself said, "Most assuredly, I say to you, before Abraham was, I AM" (John 8:58). Jesus didn't say, "Before Abraham was, I was." He said, "Before Abraham was, I AM." In other words, Abraham had history. Jesus doesn't have any; He is forever.

The Bible tells us Jesus, in His eternity, is the Creator of this world. Most people know that Genesis 1:1 says, "In the beginning God created the heavens and the earth." But the Bible also says God the Father created the world through the agency of God the Son.

John 1:3 says, "All things were made through Him, and without Him nothing was made that was made."

Colossians 1:16 says, "For by Him all things were created that are in heaven and that are on earth." The book of Hebrews begins with these words: "God…has in these last days spoken to us by His Son, whom He has appointed heir of all things, through whom also He made the worlds" (1:1-2). Think about this! The Baby born in Bethlehem was present when the world was created in Genesis 1, and He actually created the world as we see it today.

God's love for us is unending—it is eternal. Sometimes we think Jesus only loves us when we do good things. Some people think God loves them when they're good and He doesn't when they're bad. But long before the world was made, long before Adam and long before Abraham, Jesus loved us.

Many people have trouble accepting the fact that Almighty God loves them. They feel inadequate, unworthy, and guilty. Maybe you struggle to believe Jesus loves you at all, or maybe you think He loves you in varying degrees. But God, through Jesus Christ, has loved you before the foundation of the world. He has loved you from infinity with a never-ending love. Before you could do anything good or bad, you were loved by God. He doesn't love us because of who we are but because of who *He* is.

When we succeed, He says, "I love you." When we fail He says, "I love you." Because He is love, there is nothing we can ever do to make Him stop loving us. And there's nothing we can ever do to make Him love us more than He already does. Everything we've ever done or thought—whether good, bad, or indifferent—was in the future when God set His love on us. He loves us like we cannot imagine.

ETERNITY IN OUR HEART: JESUS LONGS FOR US

The Jesus who has loved us forever created us in a moment in time, and He created us with a yearning for eternity in our heart. He created us in His image, so there is a space within us only He can occupy.

The Desire for Eternal Life

Ecclesiastes 3:11 says, "He has made everything beautiful in its time. Also He has put eternity in their hearts, except that no one can find out the work that God does from beginning to end." That means everyone has a hunger and longing for God, even if we don't know it.

In our culture, people attempt to fill that vacuum with everything else. We try to find meaning through riches, relationships, pride, money, sex, drugs, or other things. Everything we stuff into that space doesn't fit because that space was made for God. He built a space in our heart that is specifically for Him. If you don't know or accept that, it doesn't go away. The yearning for Him—for something or someone beyond the transitory—is still there. Romans 8:22 says, "For we know that the whole creation groans and labors with birth pangs together until now."

We were not built for this world, and this world was not built for us. We were built for eternity. Until we get to our eternal home, we're always going to feel a bit displaced. When we get to heaven, one of the first things we're going to do is say, "Oh, this is what I've been looking for!"

The Description of Eternal Life

What, then, is eternal life? John 17:3 says, "And this is eternal life, that they may know You, the only true God, and Jesus Christ whom You have sent." Similarly, John 10:28 says, "And I give them eternal life, and they shall never perish; neither shall anyone snatch them out of My hand."

If you had to define eternal life, how would you describe it? You might talk about infinity, about having no beginning or ending. While those descriptions are correct, it's not how Jesus defined it. He said it was synonymous with knowing Him and knowing His Father.

The everlasting life Jesus promised is more than simply living forever. It's about having an endless relationship with God.

Eternal life was described by one Scottish minister as, *The Life of God in the Soul of Man*. That's an apt phrase. When we accept Jesus Christ, He occupies and fills the vacuum God created in our heart. And—this is important to understand—eternal life begins at that moment. When the Christian dies, it's just a step forward. We don't get eternal life through death; we get eternal life through faith. When we receive Jesus Christ as Savior, at that very moment, we begin the experience of eternal life.

If the followers of Christ have the experience of eternal life right now, what does that mean? First, it means enjoyment. Many nonbelievers think they don't want to be Christians because it will ruin their fun. But the greatest joy we'll ever know is becoming a Christian. Christ gives us a deep settled peace in our heart, and we know all is well between us and our Maker.

In addition to enjoyment, we have enlargement. It isn't God's purpose to shrink our life, but to expand us. He gives us the Holy Spirit, who begins to identify gifts in us that can be utilized for the kingdom. Becoming a Christian isn't dialing back life; it's turning it up. How wonderful to see how God allows us, through faith, to touch people everywhere we go and to make an impact we never thought possible!

Our present experience of eternal life also brings enrichment. When we become Christians, the Holy Spirit brings heaven into our heart. We are blessed with every spiritual blessing in the heavenly places, and the Holy Spirit is in our heart as a guarantee of what's still to come (Ephesians 1:3, 13-14). Out of the fullness of God's grace, He gives us one blessing after another. He daily loads us with benefits. When we decide to follow Christ, all those things happen in our life. That doesn't mean we don't have difficult issues and deep problems. Those, too, are a part of life, but with Christ we can deal with them from an eternal perspective.

Eternity in Heaven: Jesus Lives for Us

After Jesus rose from the dead, He appeared to His disciples over a period of forty days, then He ascended to heaven and resumed His seat of glory on the throne of God. Hebrews 10:12 says, "But this Man, after He had offered one sacrifice for sins forever, sat down at the right hand of God." That's where Jesus is right now—at the right hand of the Father. He sat down, not because He was tired but because He had finished His earthly work.

What is He doing, then, right now?

Jesus Is Providing for Us

First, Jesus is providing for us. Ephesians 1:20-21 says, "[God] raised Him from the dead and seated Him at His right hand in the heavenly places, far above all principality and power and might and dominion." At this very moment, Jesus is seated at the supreme place of authority, and He isn't resting—He is reigning. He is in charge of this world, this universe, the unfolding of events, and the tide of history. No matter how hopeless the political climate or global crises may seem, Almighty God has it all in His hands.

Nothing will happen that Jesus doesn't let happen or want to happen. He is in control. So when you go to bed tonight and are tempted to worry about what will happen tomorrow, rest assured it's all under control. It's under *His* control. We may not see it in the everyday things that go on around us, but we have it straight from the Word of God that Jesus Christ is at the right hand of the Father and He has everything in hand. Hallelujah!

Jesus Is Praying for Us

Here's the second thing—Jesus is praying for us. In Luke 22:31-32, Jesus said to Simon Peter, "Simon, Simon! Indeed, Satan has asked for you, that he may sift you as wheat. But I have prayed for you, that your faith should not fail."

If Jesus could pray effectively for Peter during His earthly ministry, can He not do the same for us now from His place on the throne? Romans 8:34 says, "Who is he who condemns? It is Christ who died, and furthermore is also risen, who is even at the right hand of God, who also makes intercession for us." Hebrews 7:25 adds, "Therefore He is also able to save to the uttermost those who come to God through Him, since He always lives to make intercession for them."

We don't know exactly how this works. But since Jesus is the infinite and eternal God, it is absolutely possible for Him to, at one and the same time, be always praying for those of His family, including each of us. He prays for us even before we know we need prayer. He knows what our needs are. If you have a job interview, a doctor's appointment, a parent-teacher conference, or whatever it is—Jesus is praying for you. When we envision that, it's a powerful encouragement to our heart and mind. It changes our perspective in life.

Jesus Is Protecting Us

Another part of our Lord's present ministry is this—He is protecting us. The book of Jude ends with a great benediction: "Now to Him who is able to keep you from stumbling, and to present you faultless before the presence of His glory with exceeding joy, to God our Savior, who alone is wise, be glory and majesty, dominion and power, both now and forever. Amen" (Jude 1:24-25).

One of Jesus' roles in heaven is to keep us from stumbling so that one day He can present us faultless before the Father. That's what He's doing in heaven. In ways beyond our knowledge, He is watching over our steps, keeping us from stumbling and falling, and protecting us from the evil one.

Jesus Is Preparing a Place for Us

Our Lord is also preparing a place for us. Jesus said, "In My Father's house are many mansions; if it were not so, I would have told you. I go to prepare a place for you. And if I go and prepare a place for you, I will come again and receive you to Myself; that where I am, there you may be also" (John 14:2-3).

Jesus is up in heaven getting our residences ready. Jesus took six days to create the world, but He's been preparing our heavenly home since the day He ascended to heaven. If you take the biblical descriptions of New Jerusalem seriously, it's a literal place—a city, a new universe, a new planet—very real and well-described, especially in Revelation 21 and 22. Yet even with those vivid biblical details, it will be beyond anything we can imagine. He is getting things ready for us, and one day we will be with Him and live with Him forever.

But remember—when does eternal life start? It starts the day, the hour, the moment, we say "Yes" to Jesus, accept Him as our Savior, and receive the gift of eternal life. The Bible says, "For the wages of sin is death, but the gift of God is eternal life in Christ Jesus our Lord" (Romans 6:23).

PERSONAL QUESTIONS

1. Read Hebrews 9:14, 1 Timothy 1:17, Romans 1:20, and Deuteronomy 33:27.

   a. What concept is shared by all these passages as it relates to God's nature?

   b. What does Ecclesiastes 3:11 tell us about this as it relates to our own heart?

   c. Now read John 3:15-16. How does the above concept of God impact our own life?

   d. After studying this lesson, when does eternal life begin? How would you demonstrate that from the Scriptures we've studied?

2. Read Ephesians 1:1-14.

   a. When did God choose us to be part of His family?

   b. List some of the blessings described in this passage that flow from that truth.

   c. What do we have to guarantee our future inheritance in heaven?

3. Look at the following passages and describe some of the present activities of Jesus Christ as He dwells in heaven:

   a. Ephesians 1:20-21

   b. Hebrews 9:24

   c. 1 John 2:1

   d. Hebrews 7:25

   e. John 14:2

4. Read Jude 1:24-25.

   a. What is Jesus able to do for you today?

   b. How is He described in this benediction?

   c. What phrase in this benediction is most encouraging to you—and why?

1. If you were writing a dictionary, what definition would you give to the word *eternity*?

2. The concept of the eternity of Jesus Christ involves what theologians call His pre-existence. Look up these Scriptures and discuss what you think they mean in this regard.

   a. John 1:1

   b. John 17:5

   c. Colossians 1:15-19

   d. Micah 5:2

   e. John 8:58

3. Why is this such an important part of biblical teaching and Christian belief?

4. If Jesus is the eternal God who descended to earth and became a man through the virgin birth, and if He rose and ascended back to heaven, what does that tell us about His past and His future?

5. What, then, is He able to do for us? See John 3:15-16; 4:14; 4:36; 5:24; 6:47. If you have a concordance, look up several references to *eternity* and *everlasting* in the Gospel of John. The preponderance of this theme is one of the most comforting discoveries in Scripture. Write the verse that means the most to you below.

6. Jesus, being now alive and on the throne of heaven, is as active as He ever was. From the lesson we've just studied, what are some of the elements of the present ministry of Christ?

7. We've learned that eternal life begins the moment we trust Christ. Is it difficult for you to think of yourself as currently possessing and enjoying eternal life?

8. In the future, what blessings are in store for us because of the eternal, incorruptible, and imperishable nature of Christ?

   a. Philippians 3:20-21

   b. 1 Corinthians 15:42-49

DID YOU KNOW?

When Jesus rose from the grave, He didn't have the same kind of body you and I now have. His resurrection body was glorified and equipped for eternity. The Bible referred to it as imperishable and incorruptible. He was able to move through walls without opening doors. He could convey Himself from one place to another by thought. His glorified body would no longer age or suffer illness or death. His body is the prototype of what our resurrection bodies will be. Philippians 3:21 says that when the Lord returns, "[He] will transform our lowly body that it may be conformed to His glorious body." How we anticipate that! Since our Lord's body was no longer an earthly body, but a heavenly body, it was fitted to return to heaven to live within the sphere for which it was created. In 1 Corinthians 9:25, we're told we'll be given an "imperishable crown" if we remain true to Christ, so that would imply an imperishable body to match the crown. And 1 Corinthians 15:42 says, "So will it be with the resurrection of the dead. The body that is sown is perishable, it is raised imperishable" (NIV).

IS HE FROM THE OLD TESTAMENT OR THE NEW TESTAMENT?

Selected Scriptures

In this lesson we learn that every aspect of our Lord's life, ministry, death, resurrection, and mission was predicted in advance throughout the books of the Old Testament.

OUTLINE

When Dr. David Murray was asked to teach Hebrew and Old Testament in a seminary, he asked himself, "Why would God have given us the majority of the Bible in the Old Testament?" The key came when Murray realized Jesus Christ answered that question Himself. He told His disciples the Old Testament was all about *Him*.[1] Murray learned what we'll discover in this lesson—Jesus is on every page of the Hebrew Scriptures, from Genesis to Malachi.

I.   **Jesus: The Seed of the Woman**

II. **Jesus: The Passover Lamb**

III. **Jesus: The Bronze Serpent**

IV. **Jesus: The Forsaken Savior**

V.   **Jesus: The Suffering Servant**

Conclusion:

1. Knowing Jesus From the Old Testament Reassures Our Faith
2. Knowing Jesus From the Old Testament Revives Our Heart
3. Knowing Jesus From the Old Testament Restores Our Hope

When His critics challenged His identity as recorded in John's Gospel, Jesus replied, "And the Father Himself, who sent Me, has testified of Me. You have neither heard His voice at any time, nor seen His form. But you do not have His word abiding in you, because whom He sent, Him you do not believe. You search the Scriptures, for in them you think you have eternal life; and these are they which testify of Me. But you are not willing to come to Me that you may have life" (John 5:37-40).

The word "Scriptures" here referred to the Old Testament, for the New Testament hadn't yet been given. Jesus was claiming that God the Father spoke of Him in the inspired pages of the Old Testament. As we study this subject in the Old Testament, we can pinpoint more than three hundred specific predictions about Christ, plus a multitude of signs, types, indications, and foreshadowings —all pointing to Him. His birth, His life, His character, His ministry, His betrayal, His death, His resurrection, and His ascension were detailed hundreds of years before they occurred.

When you read the Old Testament with Jesus in mind, everything is different. It's impossible to miss it. We realize the Hebrew Scriptures are more than a collection of stories; they present the portrait of the coming Messiah.

In this lesson we don't have time for an exhaustive study of Old Testament Messianic prophecy, but we can touch on five great examples.

JESUS: THE SEED OF THE WOMAN

The first presentation of the Gospel in the Bible occurred as early as the Garden of Eden. We find it in the third chapter of the book of Genesis—in Genesis 3:15. Theologians call this verse the *protoevangelium. Proto* means "first" and *evangelium* means "gospel." They call Genesis 3:15 the "first Gospel."

The Bible begins with the book of Genesis and its story of Creation when God spoke and the universe came into existence. He created Adam and Eve for fellowship with Himself, but they violated His command and disobeyed Him. It was a sad day for all humanity as we fell into sin. When the first couple disobeyed the commandment of God, which was given in the abundance of His blessing, God punished them. But He never gave up on them.

The Lord had already prepared a plan of redemption to take care of Adam and Eve, and to ultimately take care of us.

Genesis 3:15 is the record of what God said to Satan. It's incredible that the first promise of the coming Redeemer was spoken by God to Satan. Almighty God said in Genesis 3:15: "And I will put enmity between you and the woman, and between your seed and her Seed; He shall bruise your head, and you shall bruise His heel."

That sounds like a code, and in a sense it is. God told Satan that one day the Seed of the woman—Jesus—would come. He predicted that Satan would bruise the Messiah's heel, but the Messiah would crush Satan's head. In other words, there would be a tremendous conflict between Satan and the promised Seed of the woman. The latter would be hurt, but the former would be destroyed. Romans 16:20 says, "And the God of peace will crush Satan under your feet shortly."

When Jesus went to the cross, Satan bruised His heel. Satan thought he had won, but he didn't destroy Jesus; he just bruised His heel. The Bible says one day Jesus will come again and crush Satan's head.

With that thought in mind, read Galatians 4:4-5 which says, "But when the fullness of the time had come, God sent forth His Son, born of a woman, born under the law, to redeem those who were under the law, that we might receive the adoption as sons."

Genesis 3:15 is one of the most encouraging verses in the Bible, because it is the first promise of the Gospel. Here we get the first inkling that a Savior would come into the world to defeat Satan and bring us back to the family of God.

JESUS: THE PASSOVER LAMB

Turning to the book of Exodus, we see another picture of the coming Savior—the Passover Lamb. God's plan of redemption continues to unfold, and here we have one of the Bible's greatest types.

The early chapters of Exodus describe the conflict between Pharaoh and Moses. God hurled many plagues against the Egyptians, culminating with the night when the Lord struck down the firstborn in every home in Egypt. But among the enslaved Hebrews, a special instruction was given. Every family was to take a spotless lamb, slaughter it, and brush its blood on the doorposts and lintels of their house.

Exodus 12:12-13 says, "For I will pass through the land of Egypt on that night, and will strike all the firstborn in the land of Egypt, both man and beast; and against all the gods of Egypt I will execute judgment: I am the Lord. Now the blood shall be a sign for you on the houses where you are. And when I see the blood, I will pass over you."

That's the origin of the word *Passover*. Jewish people celebrate the night when the angel passed over the houses where the blood was on display on the doorposts. Through this vivid Old Testament story of divine deliverance, the Lord revealed His pattern and His plan. Our salvation requires the sacrifice and blood of an innocent, spotless *lamb* (Jesus). That's exactly how the ministry of Jesus was introduced 1,400 years later when John the Baptist introduced the Messiah to the world, when he said, "Behold! The Lamb of God who takes away the sin of the world!" (John 1:29)

Think of all the things John could have said. *Behold the King of Israel! Behold the Messiah! Behold the King of kings! Behold the Prince of Peace! Behold Immanuel!*

Peter later wrote, "You were not redeemed with corruptible things, like silver or gold, from your aimless conduct received by tradition from your fathers, but with the precious blood of Christ, as of a lamb without blemish and without spot" (1 Peter 1:18-19).

Just as the *lamb* in the Old Testament enabled the death angel to pass over the houses of the Israelites who displayed the blood on their doorposts, so the blood of the Lamb of God who was slain on Calvary, when applied to our heart, keeps us from the judgment of our sin and death. Our sins are covered by the precious blood shed for us.

In the Old Testament He is the Passover Lamb. In the New Testament He's the Lamb of God who takes away the sin of the world. This is arguably the most poignant description of the Person and work of the Messiah, and its truth stretches from Genesis to Revelation.

JESUS: THE BRONZE SERPENT

The book of Numbers describes one of the most vivid symbols of Christ in the Old Testament—the bronze serpent. In Numbers 21, the children of Israel grew impatient and sinned recklessly, and grumbled against Moses and against God. As discipline, the Lord sent venomous snakes among them. The people cried out to Moses, confessing their sin and begging for mercy from God. Moses prayed for the people that God would take this punishment away. The Lord spoke to Moses and told him, "Make a fiery serpent, and set it on a pole; and it shall be that everyone who is bitten, when he looks at it, shall live" (Numbers 21:8). The Bible says, "So Moses made a bronze serpent, and put it on a pole; and so it was, if a serpent had bitten anyone, when he looked at the bronze serpent, he lived" (verse 9).

Over a thousand years later, a man named Nicodemus sought out a young rabbi named Jesus of Nazareth for personal counseling. Jesus reached back into the book of Numbers and claimed that the bronze serpent was a biblical preview of His own work on the cross. He said, "And as Moses lifted up the serpent in the wilderness, even so must the Son of Man be lifted up, that whoever believes in Him should not perish but have eternal life" (John 3:14-15).

People in the wilderness looked to the serpent and they were healed. And when you and I look to Jesus, so are we. The remedy for our past sinful choices isn't to heal ourselves. The remedy is to simply look to Jesus. Look to the cross and say, "I know You're there for me. You paid the penalty for my sin." It's the perfect illustration of Jesus, and it is found in Numbers chapter 21. That is Jesus in the Old Testament.

JESUS: THE FORSAKEN SAVIOR

Let's move out of the historical books of the Old Testament and open the book of Psalms. We can discover a lot about the Lord Jesus Christ in the 150 chapters of this great book of the Bible, for many of the Psalms are Messianic in nature and have specific predictions about the coming Messiah. But we only have time in this lesson to pause at Psalm 22, which foretells the crucifixion and resurrection of Christ so accurately you would think the writer was standing at the foot of the cross. Psalm 22 predicts the words Jesus utters while dying on the cross (verse 1); the public nature of His suffering and death (verse 7); the exact words flung at Him by bystanders (verse 8); the dehydration and loss of bodily fluids involved in His death (verse 14); the disjointed position of His body (verse 14); His intense thirst (verse 15); the piercing of His hands and feet (verse 16); His unclothed state in death (verse 17); the gambling away of His garments by the executioners (verse 18); His declaration of victory at the resurrection (verse 22); and the global impact of the message of death and resurrection throughout history (verses 27-31).

All that, one thousand years in advance!—though the process of execution by crucifixion was not even invented at that time. Yet David vividly described it in this Psalm that was written ten centuries before it actually happened.

JESUS: THE SUFFERING SERVANT

Now let's move to the prophet Isaiah, whose book contains so much prophetic information about the coming Messiah we sometimes call the book of Isaiah the "Fifth Gospel." According to this prophet, the Messiah would be born of a virgin (Isaiah 7:14); He would be called *Immanuel*, which means, "God with us" (7:14); He would come from Galilee (9:1); He would be born a Child, a Son; the Prince of Peace who would inherit the throne of His father David (9:6-7); He would be anointed by the Holy Spirit (11:1-2); He would possess remarkable traits of character and personality (11:3-5); and do something so extraordinary on a mountain that the shroud of death covering all nations would be destroyed and He would swallow up death forever (25:6-8).

Isaiah wrote all about Jesus approximately seven hundred years before the Savior was born.

When you come to the great fifty-third chapter of Isaiah, you have the story of the Suffering Servant. Isaiah wrote: "But He was wounded for our transgressions, He was bruised for our iniquities; the chastisement for our peace was upon Him, and by His stripes we are healed. All we like sheep have gone astray; we have turned, every one, to his own way; and the Lord has laid on Him the iniquity of us all" (Isaiah 53:5-6).

These examples are only a portion of the Old Testament prophecies related to Jesus Christ. Mathematicians who have studied the prophecies about Christ in the Old Testament have concluded that the probability of all the predictions about Him coming true is virtually nonexistent without the hand of an omniscient God recording in advance what would happen. Jesus Christ is the promised Messiah, and there isn't any question about it. Any honest and reasonable person who studies this subject with integrity and an open mind can only be amazed at the accuracy of the fulfillments. To know the Suffering Servant of Isaiah is to know the Gospel and the extraordinary love of Jesus!

CONCLUSION

What, then, does this mean to us?

Knowing Jesus From the Old Testament Reassures Our Faith

First, when we study the fulfilled Old Testament prophecies about Christ, it tremendously strengthens our faith. Some people believe that faith is believing in something despite the evidence, but it's actually believing in something because of the evidence. The Bible tells us the truth. Whenever we have a trickle of doubt about the truthfulness of Christianity, one of the best things we can do is go back and read Psalm 22 or Isaiah 53 or spend some time in a survey or summary of Old Testament Messianic prophecy. Our faith is always reassured and affirmed, for no one except God could have made so many predictions—all of which came true exactly as stated.

Knowing Jesus From the Old Testament Revives Our Heart

Second, knowing Jesus from the Old Testament brings revival to us; it makes our heart burn. In Luke 24, two disciples were walking to the village of Emmaus on Easter Sunday, and they were troubled and confused. All of a sudden, Someone caught up with them and began walking with them. It was Jesus, but they did not recognize Him. They told Him of their hopes that Jesus would be the One to release them from their bondage. When they arrived at their home, they offered Him dinner, and as He broke the bread, they realized Who it was who had been with them.

Luke 24:32 says, "And they said to one another, 'Did not our heart burn within us while He talked with us on the road, and while He opened the Scriptures to us?'" When Jesus opened the Old Testament Scriptures concerning Himself, their hearts revived, and they were filled with joy and excitement at this truth: The Jesus of the Old Testament is the Jesus of the New Testament. He is the promised Messiah.

Knowing Jesus From the Old Testament Restores Our Hope

And then, knowing the truth about Messianic prophecy and that Jesus fulfills that calling restores our hope. Writing about the purpose of the Old Testament, the apostle Paul said: "For whatever things were written before were written for our learning, that we through the patience and comfort of the Scriptures might have hope" (Romans 15:4). We have hope. It's not a hope-so hope, it's a *know* so hope. We know that Jesus is who He claims to be.

Make sure the promised Messiah is your Savior, study His portrait, and always remember the combination to a life of joy and victory is the simplest formula in the world—it's simply J-E-S-U-S. He is the Jesus of the Old and the Jesus of the New Testaments. We find Him in the Old in prophecy and picture; we find Him in the New in presence and in power.

Most of all, we must find Him in our heart. He built a space within us only He can fill. We can try to fill it with everything else, but only Jesus satisfies us. It's not a matter of simply knowing about Him; it's a matter of knowing Him, loving Him, and walking with Him in the everyday experience of life. We were created for Him—the Jesus of the Old and New Testaments, the Jesus of eternity.

Notes

1.   David Murray, *Jesus on Every Page* (Nashville, TN: Thomas Nelson, 2013), 10-18.

2.   Peter Stoner and Robert Newman, *Science Speaks* (Chicago: Moody Press, 1958).

PERSONAL QUESTIONS

1. Read John 5:31-40.

   a. Jesus answered His critics by saying He had three sources of testimony—John the Baptist (verses 33-35); His own works and miracles (verse 36); and God the Father through the pages of the Old Testament Scriptures (verses 35-39). When the New Testament uses the word "Scriptures," to what does it refer?

   b. What do you think Jesus meant when He said the Scriptures testify of Him?

   c. In what way did the critics of our Lord fail? (verse 40)

   d. If we respond correctly to the three-fold witness of Christ, what gift do we receive? (verse 40)

2. Read Genesis 3:14-15.

   a. To whom are these statements addressed?

b. How would you explain the last part of verse 15?

3. Read 1 Peter 1:18-21.

   a. How are we redeemed?

   b. When did God decide to redeem the world in this way? (verse 20)

4. Read Psalm 22:16-31.

   a. What words indicate the great change of tone between verses 21 and 22?

   b. In what way is this predictive of the resurrection of Jesus Christ?

   c. In verse 27, who will benefit from this message?

   d. In verse 31, who else will benefit?

1. Read Genesis 3:15.

   a. How would you paraphrase this verse to highlight the Messianic nature of what God was saying to Satan?

   b. In what way was Jesus' heel bruised? Do you think this is to be taken literally?

   c. What is the significance of Satan's head being crushed? Is this a past or future event?

2. Take some time to trace the doctrine of the Lamb through the passages below. Discuss with the group how they speak to you —spiritually, emotionally, and intellectually.

   a. Genesis 4:4; 22:7

   b. Exodus 12:5

   c. Leviticus 23:12

   d. Isaiah 53:7

   e. John 1:29

   f. Acts 8:32

   g. 1 Peter 1:19

   h. Revelation 21:23

3. What should the fulfillment of these and other Messianic Scriptures tell us? See Luke 24:32-45.

4. How is this personally encouraging to you? Share your answer with the group.

5. Discuss in what way fulfilled Messianic Scripture is evidence of and a defense for the integrity of the Christian faith.

6. If the prophecies of our Lord's first coming were fulfilled so completely, how should we treat the predictions about His Second Coming?

7. Read Isaiah 53 and list five predictions that were fulfilled by Jesus when He came. Share with the group what verse in this chapter is the most compelling to you.

DID YOU KNOW?

In his book *Science Speaks*, mathematician Peter Stoner applied the mathematical principles of probability to various Old Testament predictions. Stoner selected eight Old Testament predictions relating to Christ's life and ministry and formulated the mathematical probability of their coming true in one man. The probability was equivalent to covering the state of Texas with silver dollars to a depth of two feet, then marking one of those silver dollars and dropping it somewhere into the pile, stirring it thoroughly. The chance of a blindfolded man choosing the marked silver dollar is equal to the chances of all eight of those prophecies being fulfilled in one man in history. Yet there are not eight but more than three hundred predictions.[2]

IS HE THE SON OF MARY OR THE SON OF GOD?

Philippians 3:8 and Selected Scriptures

In this lesson we learn about the dual nature of Christ. He is both human (the Son of Mary) and divine (the Son of God).

OUTLINE

Jesus is unique in human history, a Person beyond description. The Bible uses scores of names and titles to describe Him, and each speaks of a different facet of His personality or work. But the most poignant title given to Christ is *Son*. It's both personal and profound, and the mystery of His identity is found in the phrases: Son of Mary and Son of God. Through these titles, we can come to understand He is fully human yet fully God.

I. The Son of Mary
   A. The Mystery of Jesus' Birth
   B. The Measure of Jesus' Life

II. The Son of God
   A. We Need Jesus to Show Us God
   B. We Need Jesus to Save Us From Our Sins
   C. We Need Jesus to Set Us Free From Death
   D. We Need Jesus to Sympathize With Us in Our Weaknesses
   E. We Need Jesus to Strengthen Us in Times of Temptation

The Bible is where we meet Jesus Christ and study His character, His attributes, and His titles. Of all the titles attached to the person of Christ, perhaps the most meaningful is *Son*. Isaiah 9:6 says, "For unto us a Child is born, unto us a Son is given."

Jesus is called the Son of Abraham, the Son of David, the Son of Joseph, the Son of the Highest, and the Son of His love. He is called the "only begotten Son" and the "one and only Son." Jesus frequently referred to Himself as the Son of Man. Ten times in John's Gospel He is called the Son of God.

Two of our Lord's most important titles were Son of Mary and Son of God. The title Son of Mary indicates His humanity, that He was born of the virgin Mary and shares all the characteristics of humanness.

The title Son of God speaks of His deity, indicating He is equal with God. The Jewish people of Christ's day understood that the word *Son* meant "possessing the characteristics of." When Jesus called Himself "Son of God," He was telling us He had all the characteristics of God, that He was God Himself.

John 5:18 says, "Therefore the Jews sought all the more to kill Him, because He not only broke the Sabbath, but also said that God was His Father, making Himself equal with God."

With that understanding, the best place to begin studying the life of Jesus is by looking at His title of Son. Let's focus on those two elements—His role as the Son of Mary (indicating His humanity) and as the Son of God (indicating His deity).

THE SON OF MARY

When the Bible speaks of Jesus' humanity it begins with His birth and encourages us to respond with wonder and worship as did the shepherds and the Wise Men. Paul wrote to Timothy, "And without controversy great is the mystery of godliness: God was manifested in the flesh" (1 Timothy 3:16). This is the mystery of the ages, something unlike anything that had ever happened before or will ever happen again. God entered the human race through the process of a virgin who was overshadowed by the Spirit of the Almighty.

The Mystery of Jesus' Birth

The mystery of Jesus' identity is wrapped up in the reality of the virgin birth. This doctrine teaches that Jesus was divinely conceived in the womb of Mary by the Holy Spirit, bringing together His two natures, His deity and His humanity.

When Gabriel indicated this to Mary, her response was, "How can this be, since I do not know a man?" (Luke 1:34) The angel answered, "The Holy Spirit will come upon you, and the power of the Highest will overshadow you; therefore, also, that Holy One who is to be born will be called the Son of God. Now indeed, Elizabeth your relative has also conceived a son in her old age; and this is now the sixth month for her who was called barren. For with God nothing will be impossible" (Luke 1:35-37). She instantly grasped the mystery and miracle of the angel's pronouncement.

The key word is "overshadow." The idea in the language of the Bible is of a great cloud engulfing someone. When you're overshadowed, you're engulfed by something. The people of Israel used that metaphor to describe God's undeniable presence. When God came down on Mount Sinai, for example, in the book of Exodus, the mountain was overshadowed with thick and supernatural clouds. With all His creative energy, the Lord was going to surround Mary with His presence, and she would miraculously become pregnant. Joseph would not be the human father. Jesus was entering this world from the realm of eternity.

The birth of Jesus, then, was not the beginning of Jesus. He did not begin at Bethlehem. As God, He is eternal. There never was a time when Jesus was not, and there never will be a time when Jesus ceases to be. What happened at Bethlehem was that Jesus, who existed forever as God, also became a man.

Throughout history, the virgin birth of Christ has been one of the most assaulted doctrines of the Christian faith. But think of this: Jesus' mother, Mary, was human. She loved Jesus and was willing to do anything to protect Him. On the hill of Golgotha as Jesus was about to be crucified, a small group of people gathered at the foot of the hill, and His mother was there. To prevent the death of her Son, all she had to do was to step forward and say, "No, He is not the Son of God. He is the son of Joseph. I remember the night when He was conceived. Don't kill Him; He is not the Son of God. He is my son and the son of Joseph."

But Mary stood there watching her Son die, because she knew in her heart that the charge against Him was true. He was the Son of God as well as the Son of Mary. There is no other explanation for His birth.

The Measure of Jesus' Life

What about the measure of His life? Is there anything we can point to that would help us demonstrate that Jesus really was a human being, that He lived upon this earth as we humans live?

First, He did what humanity does. He was born (Luke 2:7). He grew up (Luke 2:40, 52). He had brothers and sisters (Mark 6:2-3). He grew tired (John 4:6). He got thirsty (John 19:28). He got hungry (Matthew 4:2). He became physically weak (Matthew 4:11; Luke 23:26). He died (Luke 23:46).

Second, He felt what humanity feels. As we read the four Gospels, we can't miss the range of Jesus' emotions. He felt compassion, anger, indignation, and zeal. On occasion He was troubled, distressed, sorrowful, and depressed. We see Him deeply moved and grieved. He sighed and wept and groaned. In the Garden of Gethsemane, He was in emotional agony. But on other occasions, He was surprised and amazed. He rejoiced and was full of joy. He displayed the kinds of emotions we feel today.[1]

John Calvin said, "Christ has put on our feelings as well as our flesh."[2]

Third, Jesus thought as humanity thinks. Luke 2:52 says of our Lord's adolescent years, "Jesus increased in wisdom and stature, and in favor with God and men." When it says He increased in wisdom, it means that Jesus grew intellectually in His knowledge. He learned, memorized, pondered, and developed the ability to think logically. We're led to believe He had to learn the Scriptures like we do. Notice how verse 52 indicates a four-fold maturity that should be true of every human—He grew intellectually, physically, spiritually, and socially.

No wonder Paul said the mystery of Jesus is great! He was, is, and always will be God; but at the virgin's conception, He also became a man. And during His life on earth, He was subject to certain earthly, human limitations.

When we get to heaven we'll see Jesus. We'll be able to examine the prints of the nails in His hands and the scar in His side. We can't understand all the nuances involved in that. But Jesus became a man for us. He is the Son of Mary.

THE SON OF GOD

But He is also the Son of God. This is arguably the most important title of Christ in the entire New Testament. It appears more than forty times. In the simplest of terms, "Son of God" is how the New Testament describes Jesus and His relationship to God the Father. It also shows us His divine identity. While Jesus was fully human, He was also fully God.

There never has been anyone like that. Jesus Christ is without precedent. There is no one to compare Him to. There will never be anyone like Him. He is the single, most unique important Person who's ever walked on earth. He is the individually most notable character you will ever hear about. He is God with all the power, attributes, glory, prerogatives, and capacities of God.

When Jesus stilled the storm while with the disciples, they were overcome with amazement and they worshiped Him, convinced that only God could have performed the miracle. They said, "Truly You are the Son of God" (Matthew 14:33).

At His trial before the Jewish council, His opponents charged Him with claiming to be the Son of God, which they recognized as a claim of deity. Anyone claiming to be God could be charged with blasphemy and killed. Think of it! The only valid charge they could ever come up with against Jesus was that He claimed to be the Son of God, because He was. Even the devil recognizes that Jesus is God. The demons cried out in Matthew 8:29, "What have we to do with You, Jesus, You Son of God?"

So while Jesus is just like us in every way, He is also Lord over us in every way. He is the God-Man who deserves all of our worship and all of our praise. Philippians 2:10-11 reminds us of that fact: "That at the name of Jesus every knee should bow, in heaven and on earth and under the earth, and every tongue declare that Jesus Christ is Lord, to the glory of God the Father" (NLT).

Is He then the Son of Mary or is He the Son of God? He is both. If you accept one, you must accept the other. He cannot be one without the other, because if He is one without the other, He destroys what He claims to be. And as the Son of Mary and the Son of God, He has a unique role in our life—in five different areas.

We Need Jesus to Show Us God

The Bible says in order for us to know God, we need to know Jesus because He brings God into focus for us. On one occasion, Philip, one of Jesus' disciples, said, "Lord, show us the Father." Jesus replied, "Have I been with you so long, and yet you have not known Me, Philip? He who has seen Me has seen the Father; so how can you say, 'Show us the Father'?" (John 14:8-9)

In other words, Jesus was saying, "I am the God you want to know. I am the Father who can be seen. I am the One who came to show you the Father." When we study Jesus we're getting to know God. He is the One who shows us who God is and what God is like.

We Need Jesus to Save Us From Our Sins

Second, because Jesus is both man and God, He can save us from our sins. First Timothy 2:5-6 says, "For there is one God and one Mediator between God and men, the Man Christ Jesus, who gave Himself a ransom for all, to be testified in due time."

Jesus said, "I am the way, the truth and the life. No one comes to the Father except through Me" (John 14:6). He is the one way to God. In Jesus Christ, we have a perfect and true Mediator since He possesses the nature and attributes of God and the nature and attributes of man. He is the God-Man and, therefore, the only One who could righteously and perfectly bring peace to these two warring parties. Jesus Himself said that He had come to this earth for this very reason. Luke 19:10 says, "For the Son of Man has come to seek and to save that which was lost."

Only Jesus can save us from our sins.

We Need Jesus to Set Us Free From Death

The dual nature of Christ also gives Him the prerogative to set us free from death. Hebrews 2:14-15 says, "Since the children have flesh and blood, he too shared in their humanity so that by his death he might break the power of him who holds the power of death—that is, the devil—and free those who all their lives were held in slavery by their fear of death" (NIV).

Jesus became the Son of Mary and took upon Himself flesh and blood so He could do what we could never do. He confronted Satan and destroyed him. Satan is a defeated and disarmed enemy, and his greatest weapon—death—has been rendered powerless by the resurrection of Jesus Christ.

The Bible says, "For this purpose the Son of God was manifested, that He might destroy the works of the devil" (1 John 3:8). The way He could destroy him was to rob him of his weapon—death. Physical death, spiritual death, eternal death. Jesus took away Satan's weapon of death by dying and rising again. He defeated the power of death over us once and for all.

For a Christian now, death is just a shadow. No longer is it the true substance of our fear; it's just a momentary obscuring of the light.

We Need Jesus to Sympathize With Us in Our Weaknesses

The fourth reason why it's important to understand that Jesus is both the Son of God and the Son of Mary is because that mysterious union of natures allows Him to sympathize with our weaknesses. Hebrews 4:15 says, "For we do not have a High Priest who cannot sympathize with our weaknesses."

We can't really understand what someone is going through until we go through something like it ourselves. Jesus became one of us so that He could sympathize with our weaknesses and understand our struggles. Life is difficult at times, but there is nothing we'll ever experience that Jesus doesn't understand.

We Need Jesus to Strengthen Us in Times of Temptation

Finally, the dual nature of Jesus enables Him to provide strength to us in times of temptation. C. S. Lewis said it this way, "We never find the strength of the evil impulse inside us until we try to fight it; and Christ, because He was the only man who never yielded to temptation, is also the only man who knows to the full what temptation means."[3]

Because He experienced the power of temptation and overcame it, we can confidently trust Him to help us. "For in that He Himself has suffered, being tempted, He is able to aid those who are tempted" (Hebrews 2:18).

The question is: Who is Jesus to you? Is He your Savior? He is the only One who can help you in your weakness and give you victory over your temptations. For all who come to Him, the offer of heaven and an eternity with God awaits. He is our Lord and God. He is the Father's Son and the Son of Mary. He is unique in human history. He is the *Jesus You May Not Know!*

Notes

1. G. Walter, "Emotions of Jesus," *Christianity Today*, February 3, 1997.

2. David Matthis, "Jesus is Fully Human," *Desiring God*, December 15, 2016.

3. C. S. Lewis, *Mere Christianity* (MacMillan, 1952), 124-125.

PERSONAL QUESTIONS

1. Read John 1:14-18, which deals with the unique nature of the Lord's identity.

   a. Who is referred to in verse 14 as the Word? (See also verse 1.)

   b. According to verse 14, what did He do?

   c. What do we see when we look at Jesus? (verse 14)

   d. According to verse 16, what does He give us?

   e. According to verse 18, what does the presence of Jesus mean to us?

2. According to John 5:18, why did Jesus' enemies seek to kill Him?

3. Read 1 Timothy 2:1-7.

   a. What does God want for every individual (verse 4)?

b. How is Jesus described in verse 5?

c. What did He do according to verse 6?

d. According to verse 7, what should we do about that?

4. Read Hebrews 2:9-18.

   a. In verse 9, we're told that Jesus was made a little lower than the angels. What do you think that means?

   b. What title is given to Jesus in verse 10?

   c. What does He call us in verse 11?

   d. How did Jesus destroy Satan's work according to verse 14?

   e. How specifically can this be a help to you today? (See verse 18.)

GROUP QUESTIONS

1. Read Luke 1:26-38.

   a. Has the doctrine of the virgin birth ever troubled you, or have you encountered people who questioned the virgin birth of Christ?

   b. Discuss why this truth is so important.

   c. How is Jesus described in verses 31-33?

   d. When Mary asked how this could be since she had never known a man, the angel appealed to a special ministry of the Holy Spirit. What does verse 35 tell us about the ultimate identity of Jesus Christ?

   e. How does verse 37 remind us that the virgin birth is a logical possibility given a belief in God?

   f. How does Mary's answer serve as a lesson for all of us?

2. Read Philippians 2:1-16.

   a. How is Jesus described in the first part of verse 6? Discuss what you think that means.

   b. What did He do in verse 7?

   c. And in verse 8?

   d. According to verse 9, what happened to Him afterward?

   e. Because of that, there are two things we must do. The first is given in verses 10-11, and the second is given in verses 14-16. List these two obligations and give some thought to them. In what way can we improve our lives today by following the example of Jesus in these specific ways?

J esus made a supernatural entrance into the world and a supernatural exit from it. He wasn't born like others, and He didn't die like others. His pre-existence as God is eternal. When He entered humanity through the womb of a virgin, He became both God and Man. After His crucifixion, He rose from the dead, being transformed and glorified incorruptibly for heaven, and He ascended through the sky back to His throne. That's what we would expect from a supernatural Savior. Our Lord's life was so well crafted and choreographed that only heaven could have designed it!

IS HE THE TEACHER OF TRUTH OR THE TRUTH TO BE TAUGHT?

Selected Scriptures

In this lesson we learn about the teaching ministry of Jesus. Everything He taught was true because He Himself was the personification of Truth— Truth that has the power to transform us.

OUTLINE

Jesus said, "I am . . . the truth" (John 14:6). Our Lord always spoke the truth because truth itself originated with Him. God is, by definition, ultimate Truth. Jesus was the literal personification of Truth. Though we live in an age where people deny the absolute nature of truth, the Christian faith is founded on Him who was and is the Truth; and whose teachings always challenge, change, and cheer us.

I. **Jesus: The Truth**

II. **Jesus: The Teacher**
   A. His Teaching Will Challenge You
   B. His Teaching Will Change You
   C. His Teaching Will Cheer You

Teachers change lives. Millions of people have been influenced by a great teacher they sat under in grade school, high school, college, or Sunday school. Good teachers leave a deep imprint. We can all think back over our lives and remember a handful of teachers who hold a revered place in our memories. Educators need to remember they are following in the footsteps of Jesus Christ. He was often addressed, not as *Jesus* or *Christ* or *Lord*, but by His title of *Teacher*. He was called *Teacher* or *Rabbi* more than 45 times in the New Testament.

Jesus also spoke of Himself in this way. In John 13:13, He told the disciples, "You call Me Teacher and Lord, and you say well, for so I am."

The word *disciple* was used in the New Testament to describe His followers, and it literally means "learners." They were learning from the best—literally the best Teacher the world has ever seen. When we speak of discipleship, we're talking about learning. We are the students of Jesus.

Just as Christ is King of kings and Lord of lords, He is the Teacher of teachers—the supreme educator of the ages. Sometimes He taught one or two or three people at a time; other times He spoke to thousands at once without amplification or electronic projection. Even now, He speaks across the ages, and His words reach the deepest foundations of our mind and heart. Whenever you open the Bible, you're sitting at His feet just like the disciples of yesteryear. We know His teachings are true because He Himself is the Truth.

Before we look at the nature of His teachings, let's look at what it means for Jesus to be the very definition of Truth.

JESUS: THE TRUTH

Jesus is the Truth, which relates to the fact He is both God and Man. As God, He is the source of the Truth; as Man, He is the personification of the Truth. In John 14:6, He said, "I am the way, the truth, and the life. No one comes to the Father except through Me."

He didn't simply say, "I will show you the way, I will tell you the truth, I will provide you with life." He boldly declared He was those things. He is the very embodiment of those realities.

The concept of truth is a major theme in John's Gospel and in his other writings as well. As we study the fourth Gospel, we can't help but to notice how this subject keeps coming up. John begins his Gospel by calling Jesus Christ the "true Light" who came from the Father "full of grace and truth" (John 1:9, 14).

Why was John so moved by the nature of truth? Perhaps his interest was prompted by something he heard when Jesus was on trial. Standing before the Roman governor, Pontius Pilate, Jesus said, "Everyone who is of the truth hears My voice."

Pilate snapped back, asking cynically, "What is truth?" (John 18:37-38)

That is still the contemptuous cry of relativism, humanism, and secularism today. Pilate's question has overtaken our society. Most modern thinkers reject the existence of ultimate truth or absolute values. The scornful words of Pilate are echoing in the halls of our colleges, across our screens, through the pages of our textbooks, and the world tells us there are no eternal and final foundations.

John adamantly declared that Jesus Christ is the communication of truth. Without this core axiom, there's nothing on which to build one's life. That's why there's so much chaos and confusion in our world today. Everyone's inventing their own variety of truth. That leads to the kind of despair that possibly overwhelmed Pilate, who has gone down in history as one of the greatest fools who ever lived. He stood face to face with the Truth Himself and rejected Him. He had the Truth standing in front of him and he asked the Truth, "What is truth?"

If only Pilate had understood it like this: If there is a God, He would by definition have to be truthful in every way, or else He would be flawed and therefore not God at all. If He is truthful in every way, He is the Creator of truth, the Source of truth, the Possessor of truth, the Professor of truth, and the Judge of truth. His words, by logical necessity, would be true and trustworthy. It would therefore be reasonable to speak of ultimate truth and absolute morality in the universe.

If Jesus Christ is the Incarnation of truth, it logically follows that we can have a personal relationship with Him who is the embodiment of Truth. In knowing Jesus, we can know Truth. The truth is absolute and objective, but it's also personal and knowable. That's why Jesus said, "And you shall know the truth, and the truth shall make you free" (John 8:32).

Because this Truth is a Person, you can know Him; and because He is Jesus, He can set you free. Nothing is more liberating than that.

Today in our culture our greatest need is for truth, for honest reporting, for honest speaking, for truthful living.

The Bible says there's only one Person who can give us that truth, that way, that life—and that is Jesus Christ. You will never have a genuine moment of truth until you meet the Truth Himself, the Lord Jesus.

JESUS: THE TEACHER

Going back to the question, "Is He the teacher of the truth or is He the truth itself?" the answer, of course, is He is both. Because He is the latter, He must also be the former. Because He is the embodiment of truth, He must speak truthfully, and His words must be trustworthy. And what a teacher He is! We can learn so much about Jesus and about ourselves by studying His matchless teaching!

The most effective teachers in life are those who model the truth that they teach and challenge their students to grow beyond what they think is possible. Jesus influenced His disciples, not only by what He said but also by how He lived and by the curriculum He taught. He had a vision of what His disciples could be, and He devoted Himself to teaching them accordingly. There are three ways Jesus' teaching affected those who heard Him, and these three ways are available to us today.

His Teaching Will Challenge You

First, when Jesus taught, His teaching challenged people; and His teaching challenges us. The Jesus you may not know was a Teacher who constantly challenged His listeners about their priorities, their potential, and their possibilities. For example, Jesus challenged the rich young ruler's priorities, telling him, in effect, "Go and sell everything you have and then come back and follow Me" (Luke 18:22).

Jesus wasn't so concerned about whether the man sold everything he had. Our Lord knew the man's real problem. The young man didn't have his wealth; his wealth had him. Jesus wanted to find out if he was willing to walk away from his fleeting possessions and seek first the kingdom.

On another occasion, Jesus sent His disciples to accomplish things that seemed beyond their potential, like feeding five thousand people, healing the sick, and casting out demons. On one occasion, they came back and said, in effect, "Lord what do we do now? It didn't work!" It was a teaching moment for Jesus and His disciples.

When Jesus gave the Great Commission, it was physically impossible for His eleven surviving disciples to complete it. But He used His words to expand their vision and to launch them into the process of planting churches around the world.

We're still following the impossible teachings of Jesus, but by His grace the impossible becomes possible.

Perhaps the most challenging part of our Lord's teaching is from the Sermon on the Mount in Matthew 5–7. These chapters prove Jesus was more than a carpenter, more than a preacher, and more than a mere man. From His first word, He spoke as if He were the Author and Interpreter of Scripture.

His words and their tone amazed the crowds, as they astound us today. In the Sermon on the Mount we have a set of ethics that have stood the test of time, a set of images that have never been forgotten, and a set of instructions so relevant and challenging for us today, it's as if they were written especially for us.

There are 111 verses in the Sermon on the Mount, and they include the Beatitudes, the Lord's Prayer, the Golden Rule, the City on a Hill, the Salt of the Earth, the Narrow Gate, and the wise man who built his house upon a rock. In this sermon we discover the eternal dimensions of morality and spirituality. We learn how to deal with anger, lust, divorce, retaliation, anxiety, oaths, and hypocrisy. All of these are taught in the Sermon on the Mount, and we know what to do when we read them.

In Matthew 5 through 7 we have the greatest advice ever given, in the greatest sermon ever preached, by the greatest Man who ever lived. The Sermon on the Mount provides evidence for the truthfulness of Christ and Christianity. For if Jesus were any less than He claimed to be, His message would have been less than it was. But He is Truth, and this sermon is still the greatest sermon from the greatest Preacher who ever lived. It's also regarded as one of the most famous speeches in world history, and the greatest message on practical ethics and moral psychology that has ever been delivered.

In this sermon, Jesus said, "Let your light so shine before men, that they may see your good works and glorify your Father in heaven" (Matthew 5:16).

He said, "But I say to you, love your enemies, bless those who curse you, do good to those who hate you, and pray for those who spitefully use you and persecute you" (Matthew 5:44).

He said, "But you, when you pray, go into your room, and when you have shut your door, pray to your Father who is in the secret place" (Matthew 6:6).

He said, "Lay up for yourselves treasures in heaven" (Matthew 6:20).

He said, "Therefore I say to you, do not worry about your life" (Matthew 6:25). And, "Seek first the kingdom of God and His righteousness. . . . Do not worry about tomorrow" (Matthew 6:33-34).

And on and on—a galaxy of commands about our attitudes, our actions, and our ambitions in life.

It's hard to imagine so much incredible truth packed into one sermon by one Person at a specific time and place in history. It's a sanctifying challenge to frequently revisit the Sermon on the Mount, working our way through it verse by verse. But when we do, we'll find verses we want to follow, for this sermon tells us how to be more like the One who is the Truth.

His Teaching Will Change You

Like no other teacher in history, Jesus' words inspire us to change, to be different, to be better, and to grow in maturity. When we read about His life and study His words, we want to be more like Him, the perfect picture of what it means to be a holy, healthy human being. •

Only one Person ever successfully lived the Christian life— Christ Himself. We read in 2 Corinthians 3:18: "But we all, with unveiled face, beholding as in a mirror the glory of the Lord, are being transformed into the same image from glory to glory, just as by the Spirit of the Lord."

When Jesus returned to heaven, He sent His Holy Spirit to earth and into the hearts of His followers to indwell them. One of the primary jobs of the indwelling Spirit is to convict us of sin and to help us grow into the likeness of Jesus. Through the Holy Spirit's work within us, we become the quiet people of God who live out the reality of the Lord Jesus Christ in our lives before a watching world.

As we notice Him doing that, we're often surprised because we start learning we are ourselves, yet not ourselves. That's the paradox of the Christian life. We see the Lord Jesus doing things in us that we never dreamed we would ever do. As we keep our eyes on Jesus, the Holy Spirit transforms us into the very person of Christ. We reflect His personality, attitudes, wisdom, love, and qualities.

Romans 8:29 says God wants us "to be conformed to the image of His Son." And Ephesians 4:15 tells us to "grow up in all things into Him who is the head—Christ." As that process unfolds within us, our life becomes more intrinsically truthful, more authentic, and more noted for its integrity because we are becoming like the One of Whom we speak.

Think of it this way: Most people in the world who perform reasonably well at their daily jobs can live however they want, within reason, during their time off the clock. Nobody finds out, nobody cares. As long as your job isn't affected, your employer doesn't care if you cheat on your spouse or argue with your neighbors. But that's not true for followers of Christ.

We should have a consistency to our lives that rings true 24 hours a day. We can't pretend to be one way, say, at church, then live however we want during the week. The consistent, continual stream of God's truth gives us constant stability in our ethics, our morality, and our personalities. We all know we're not perfect. We make mistakes. But as we grow in the Truth, our lives grow in their consistent Christlike, or Christian qualities.

His Teaching Will Cheer You

The teachings of Jesus do something else for us. They cheer us. Life is hard, but Jesus and the truths He taught give us uplifting comfort and cheer. How often have we quoted John 14:1-3: "Let not your heart be troubled; you believe in God, believe also in Me. In My Father's house are many mansions; if it were not so, I would have told you. I go to prepare a place for you. And if I go and prepare a place for you, I will come again and receive you to Myself; that where I am, there you may be also"?

It was also Jesus who said, "Peace, be still!" in Mark 4:39. And in the aforementioned Sermon on the Mount, He said, "Therefore do not worry. . . . For your heavenly Father knows that you need all these things" (Matthew 6:31-32).

Throughout His teaching, you can find this phrase, "Be of good cheer."

His promises and prophecies about the future assure us of everlasting life in a place of unending health and happiness. As we read His words in the Gospels and His inspired Word from Genesis to Revelation, we have never-ending comfort, cheer, encouragement, hope, and reassurance.

When His "red letters" are "read letters," they lift us above the aches of earth and set our eyes on things above. No one ever spoke as He did about the lilies of the field, the sparrows of the air, the storms, and the stillness. His words comfort mourners by the grave, invalids in their beds, saints in their sorrows, outcasts in their solitude—and you and me. It's amazing how the Lord Jesus gives us the very passages and verses we need for the troubles and trials of life.

As we are cheered by the Lord Jesus, our cups overflow—and so does our influence. The more we become like Christ, the more we'll be able to offer comfort and cheer to others. All of us are teachers in some way or another, and there's no better model for teachers than the great Teacher Himself. He didn't just communicate truth. He changed lives.

We cannot walk with Jesus the way He intended without being challenged, changed, and comforted. The easiest way is to open your Bible and begin reading it. Read and reread the Gospels. The greatest resource we have is God's unique Book, given to us, inspired by His Spirit, focused on His Son. The devil tries to push the Bible to the circumference of our lives so that it can't make an impact on us. But remember—the Bible is all about Jesus. And Jesus is Truth—truth that challenges us, changes us, and cheers us.

1. Read John 1:1-17, the prologue of the Gospel of John.

   a. According to verse 9, what kind of light was Jesus?

   b. According to verse 14, Jesus was full of _____ and _____.

   c. In verse 17, what did Jesus bring into the world?

2. In John 4:23, what kind of worshipers does God want us to be?

3. In John 8:16, how did Jesus describe His judgment? And what did Jesus say about His followers in John 8:32?

4. Just as the Gospel of John emphasizes the topic of truth, Jesus Himself called Himself the Truth—the personification of Truth—in John 14:6. What does that mean to you mentally and emotionally?

5. In this lesson, we've learned that when we study the truth of Jesus, we'll be challenged. What statement of Jesus has been the most challenging to you?

6. Read Ephesians 4:15. What process does God use to help us "grow up in all things" unto Christ?

7. The words of Jesus cheer us. Do you have a favorite saying from the lips of Jesus?

a. Can you think of someone who could use a word of comfort or cheer today?

b. Which of our Lord's statements would meet their need?

c. What is an appropriate way for you to share it with them?

GROUP QUESTIONS

1. In our world of "fake news" and misinformation, discuss how we can know what to trust and what not to trust? Do you find it difficult to discern the truth?

2. Read John 8:32. Discuss how we can know the Truth. In what way will it set us free?

3. How then can we find the Source of truth? (See John 8:44-46.)

4. Of all the teachings of Jesus with which you're familiar, which is the most challenging for you personally to live and obey? Why is that?

5. Read John 17:17. Discuss what the word "sanctify" means to you.

   a. According to Jesus, how are we sanctified?

   b. How do you think this process works in practical terms?

6. Based on this lesson, list some commands of Jesus that, if we took them seriously, would change us for the better.

7. In light of this study, why can Jesus cheer us like no one else can?

8. Share with the group some precepts or promises from Jesus that bring you particular comfort, joy, or cheer.

9. What single saying of Jesus would you like to share with the group today?

DID YOU KNOW?

Fact-checking has been a recognized career choice since the 1920s, when *Time* magazine hired people to preview each issue of their magazine for truth and accuracy. Many of these fact-checkers later became writers, editors, and publishers. Now fact-checking has become part of every major organization and outlet, and no detail is too small to check. In India, it was reported that a variety of apples had been named for Prime Minister Modi. Fact-checkers were quick to learn they had really been named after a renowned painter and sculptor. But here's the big question for our society: Who's checking the fact-checkers?

IS HE SEEKING US OR ARE WE SEEKING HIM?

John 4:1-42

In this lesson we learn how Jesus seeks to win others to Himself and how we can become part of that wonderful process.

OUTLINE

If we have a desire to seek Jesus Christ, it's only because He has been seeking us first. He came to seek and to save those who are lost. He was sent from heaven on a mission to search out and find those needing salvation, and to provide it by His own death and resurrection. One of the most vivid examples of our Lord's evangelistic efforts is recorded in John 4, when He traveled through Samaria to reach the woman by the well at Sychar. As we study this story, we learn how we too can seek others and share the Gospel with them.

I. **How Jesus Seeks Us**
    A. He Seeks Past the Racial Divide
    B. He Seeks Past the Social Divide
    C. He Seeks Past the Cultural Divide
    D. He Seeks Past the Moral Divide

II. **How Jesus Saves Us**
    A. He Identifies With Our Humanity
    B. He Invites Our Curiosity
    C. He Insists on Our Honesty
    D. He Invalidates Our Religiosity
    E. He Initiates Our Responsibility

III. **How Jesus Sends Us**

J esus goes above and beyond to seek and to save what is precious to Him—sinners like us. The Gospel of John is full of stories about how Jesus connected with certain individuals for whom He was burdened. The apostle John seemed to specialize in extended stories that tell us how Jesus connected with Nicodemus (chapter 3), the man by the pool of Bethesda (chapter 5), and the man blind from birth (chapter 9). One of the most gripping accounts is in chapter 4—the story of the Samaritan Woman, or, as she is sometimes called, the Woman at the Well. This story is notable because Jesus crossed a number of barriers as He went above and beyond to seek her, save her, and send her.

Samaria was a rugged patch of mountains between Judea and Galilee, and, as we'll see, Jewish travelers avoided it. There was a long history of enmity between the Jews and the Samaritans. Yet Jesus seemed to have a special place in His heart for Samaria and for this Samaritan woman who became a crucial link in spreading the Gospel throughout that region.

John 4 provides one of the Bible's best examples of soul-winning, and in this chapter we learn how to cross barriers to seek others and lead them to Christ. Our Lord has a three-fold plan for our life: He seeks us; He saves us; and He sends us.

HOW JESUS SEEKS US

Several years ago there was a lot of discussion about whether churches should be seeker-sensitive or seeker-driven. But Romans 3:11 reminds us, "There is none who understands; there is none who seeks after God." The only way we can seek Him is if He first seeks us. Remember what 1 John 4:19 says? "We love Him because He first loved us."

Jesus is the great Seeker. Luke 19:10 says, "For the Son of Man has come to seek and to save that which was lost." We may think we're seeking Jesus; but before we seek Him, He has been seeking us. We have a vivid example of this in John 4, when Jesus sought out a lost and immoral woman in Samaria. This chapter shows us how Jesus seeks us no matter where we are, what we are, or who we are. Jesus has no boundaries in His determination to bring us to Himself.

He Seeks Past the Racial Divide

Jesus seeks us past racial divisions. John 4:3-6 says, "He left Judea and departed again to Galilee. But He needed to go through Samaria. So He came to a city of Samaria which is called Sychar. . . . Now Jacob's well was there. Jesus therefore, being wearied from His journey, sat thus by the well. It was about the sixth hour."

In traveling from Judea to Galilee, the direct route would have taken Jesus through the mountainous region of Samaria. But the Jews hated the Samaritans and typically refused to travel through their land. Jewish pilgrims in those days detoured along the eastern bank of the Jordan River to avoid Samaria. Going from Jerusalem to Galilee, they would go down to Jericho, hike up the Jordan Valley, and turn westward to the Galilean region.

Bitterness between Jews and Samaritans went back centuries. In 721 B.C., the Assyrians invaded the Northern Kingdom of Israel and swept most of the Israelites into captivity, marching them to Assyria. The Assyrians repopulated the region with non-Jewish settlers. The Israelites who survived the invasion and deportation became racially intermixed with these Gentiles and their pagan religious practices.

In 587 B.C., the Babylonians destroyed the Southern Kingdom of Judah and led the survivors into captivity. But even in captivity, these Judean Jews never married Babylonians or lost their distinct Hebrew pedigree. When they returned to their homeland, the Southern Jews rejoiced in their racial distinctiveness and reviled the descendants of the Northern Kingdom who had become intermixed with Gentile blood. This led to hostility and prejudice. The Jews of Judea wanted nothing to do with the people of Samaria. They would rather walk an extra hundred miles than venture into their region. In John 4, however, Jesus traveled into this area on His way from Judea to Galilee, and His route led Him through the city of Sychar.

Jesus was an orthodox Jewish Rabbi, yet He marched into Samaria to meet a Samaritan woman, though she knew nothing about Him and wasn't even seeking Him. He was seeking her, and He didn't see her as a Samaritan but as a sinner who needed a Savior. He saw her as a person for whom He would die.

How we need the same attitude! The color of our skin or our particular family tree is immaterial. We're all sinners who need a great Savior. He died for all the world. He died for people of every tribe and tongue. Like Jesus, we need to cross racial barriers to touch needy people.

He Seeks Past the Social Divide

The racial barrier wasn't the only one Jesus crossed. A massive social wall existed between Him and the Samaritan woman. John 4:7-8 says, "A woman of Samaria came to draw water. Jesus said to her, 'Give Me a drink.' For His disciples had gone away into the city to buy food."

In that culture, Jewish men wouldn't speak to women in public. They wouldn't even talk to their wives or sisters in public. Some of the Pharisees didn't look at women in public. When they passed a woman on the street, they trained themselves to close their eyes.

Yet here was Jesus, seeking out the Samaritan woman and talking with her as naturally as one would speak to a friend. As we study the life of Christ, we're amazed at His interactions with women. Think of Mary, Martha, Mary Magdalene, the woman with the issue of blood, the widow of Nain, the woman caught in adultery, the daughter of Jairus, and the women in Luke 8 who helped finance His ministry.

To Jesus, every man, woman, and child is important. He never lets social barriers stand in His way. His interactions with women shocked the religious leaders of His day, but He came to offer Himself to the totality of the human family—to both men and women.

He Seeks Past the Cultural Divide

Jesus also seeks past cultural divisions. John 4:9 says, "The woman of Samaria said to Him, 'How is it that You, being a Jew, ask a drink from me, a Samaritan woman?' For Jews have no dealings with Samaritans." In the right sort of way, Jesus was a rule breaker, a cultural revolutionary.

Jews lived very differently from Samaritans. The social customs were different; the accents were different; the food was different; the dress was different; the climate of the towns was different. Even the landscape and scenery were different. So were the religious customs. Most Jews would have felt some culture shock venturing through the Samaritan region.

But Jesus created the whole world, and He's at home in any region. Culture divides don't exist for Him. Every town and city, every home and hovel, is populated by people needing what only He can offer. Should we not look at this world of lost men and women and realize nothing matters except showing them Christ? Tell them about Jesus! Help them know how to go to heaven. That's what Jesus did.

He Seeks Past the Moral Divide

Finally, Jesus seeks us past moral divides. Jesus was a Rabbi, a teacher. According to this passage, the Samaritan woman was living in an immoral relationship. She'd been married to five different men and was currently living with a sixth man who wasn't her husband. Yet here was the holiest man who ever lived, the Lord Jesus Christ, sitting at a well and speaking freely with her as though He was having a conversation among equals. Jesus broke through the moral divide as He pursued this Samaritan woman. Why? He didn't come to save those who are supposedly holy. He came to save sinners.

In Mark 2:17, Jesus said, "Those who are well have no need of a physician, but those who are sick. I did not come to call the righteous, but sinners, to repentance." He didn't come to make religious people better; He came to make sinners saints. In Luke 5:32, He said, "I have not come to call the righteous, but sinners, to repentance."

The Jesus you may not know gladly broke all kinds of barriers to make new friends. He crossed racial, social, cultural, and moral divides in seeking to save the lost.

We all have some unconfessed—perhaps unrecognized—prejudices. It's easy in today's culture to be discriminatory. Sometimes we run across people we simply don't like. If we're going to seek the lost as Jesus did, we have to overcome those barriers and take the Gospel to Jerusalem, Judea, Samaria, and the ends of the earth.

Jesus set the tone for all the racial issues people want to talk about today. For Him, there is only one point of division: Some people are saved by grace and others need to be. That's how Jesus seeks us, and that's how we're to seek others.

HOW JESUS SAVES US

Now we want to notice how Jesus saves us. As the story in John 4 continues, we discover some of the techniques Jesus used to build rapport with this woman and bring her to Himself. This is one of the Bible's most definitive stories about evangelism. Many teachers have used the elements of John 4 to show others how to build bridges, craft conversations, and present truth that will bring people to saving faith.

He Identifies With Our Humanity

Jesus began by asking the woman for a drink of water. He sat by the well because He was weary from walking such a distance. He sent the disciples into Sychar to buy food. We get the impression Jesus was hungry, thirsty, and tired. Notice the vivid way in which our Lord's humanity was on display. That allowed the Samaritan woman to identify with Him—not as God, but as a fellow human being. She too knew what it was to be hungry, thirsty, and tired. We all do.

When God Almighty wanted to send love to us from heaven He didn't send it in a book. He didn't send it in the Holy Spirit. He sent His love to us in a human being—Someone like us. He sent the gift in a way we could understand. We identify with Jesus. We see Him as we see ourselves, though He was pure and sinless. If Jesus had arrived in Sychar that day in His blazing majesty, He would have petrified this woman. He couldn't have had the kind of conversation that unfolded in this passage. She would have retreated from His presence.

God appeared to her in a way she could relate to. That's how He comes to us too, and that's how we ought to go to others. If others get the idea we think we're somehow superior, we can't win them. If we act "holier than thou," we'll drive them away. We have to identify with them as fellow humans with needs and desires like anyone else.

He Invites Our Curiosity

The passage continues: "Jesus answered and said to her, 'If you knew the gift of God, and who it is who says to you, "Give Me a drink," you would have asked Him, and He would have given you living water.' The woman said to Him, 'Sir, You have nothing to draw with, and the well is deep. Where then do You get that living water? Are You greater than our father Jacob, who gave us the well, and drank from it himself, as well as his sons and his livestock?' Jesus answered and said to her, 'Whoever drinks of this water will thirst again, but whoever drinks of the water that I shall give him will never thirst. But the water that I shall give him will become in him a fountain of water springing up into everlasting life'" (John 4:10-14).

Jesus engaged her curiosity. She wasn't sure what He meant, but His words resonated with her. He wasn't yet pressing her for a decision; He was drawing her into conversation. His words were curious and thought-provoking. He was patiently allowing her to see her own need.

Have you noticed how Jesus was a master at using His surroundings to preach the Gospel? On the mountainside, He pointed to the birds of the air and the lilies of the fields. He talked to fishermen about fishing for men. He was aware of His surroundings and His listeners, and He knew how to draw connections to lead them to the Good News.

Learning to make conversation and guide it toward the Gospel is a biblical method for gaining a hearing for the Good News of Christ.

He Insists on Our Honesty

In saving us, Jesus also insists on our honesty. It's not easy to draw people to a point of confessing their sins, but Jesus knew how to do it. When the Samaritan woman expressed interest in His message, Jesus replied, "Go, call your husband, and come here" (verse 16). With omniscient insight, He knew about this woman and He used His words to draw out her true situation. She replied, "I have no husband"(verse 17). Jesus said, in effect, "That is true. You've had five husbands, and now you're living with a sixth man."

We can only imagine how shocked the woman felt. After perhaps thinking a moment, she gave a safe reply, "Sir, I perceive that You are a prophet" (verse 19).

She was right about that. He was a prophet and more than a prophet! This woman had never before met Jesus, yet He knew her life's story. He wasn't trying to intimidate, insult, or embarrass her. She had obviously lived a difficult life, and He was sensitive to that. But it was necessary for her to reveal her true thirst. If living water was going to mean anything to this woman, she needed to be honest about her moral failures. If she was going to be able to appreciate God's forgiveness, she had to be honest about her life. Anyone who wants to become a Christian must be willing to confess his or her sins before God.

Many people hope they're going to heaven because they're trying to live a "good life." But from the perspective of a holy God, "There is none who does good, no, not one" (Romans 3:12). Until we come to Christ and acknowledge our emptiness without Him, we cannot be saved. What does it mean to sin? The Bible says, "For all have sinned and fall short of the glory of God" (Romans 3:23). Sin is falling short of the perfection and glory and holiness of God. And we all fall short.

He Invalidates Our Religiosity

The next part of the conversation by Jacob's well is quite interesting. When Jesus brought the woman's past up, she wasn't eager to talk about it. She changed the subject. Jesus was talking to her about her sin, and when He struck too close to home she said, in paraphrase, "Oh, You're a prophet. Well, let me ask You a question. We Samaritans worship here on this mountain, and the Jews worship in Jerusalem. What's Your opinion?"

Jesus didn't dismiss her question, but in answering it He circled back to her, saying, "Woman, believe Me, the hour is coming when you will neither on this mountain, nor in Jerusalem, worship the Father. You worship what you do not know; we know what we worship. . . . But the hour is coming, and now is, when the true worshipers will worship the Father in spirit and truth; for the Father is seeking such to worship Him" (verses 21-23).

Notice that word "seeking." God was seeking to make this woman His worshiper, and Jesus was calling her to be a true worshiper, one who worshiped in Spirit and in truth.

He Initiates Our Responsibility

The Lord then came back to His main point and initiated her responsibility. In John 4:25, He again confronted her with the truth. The woman said that one day the Messiah would come and answer everyone's questions.

That's when Jesus made a stunning statement: "I who speak to you am He" (verse 26). This is an incredible Bible moment! The Samaritan woman was discovering her responsibility, and it was personal and spiritual, not traditional and religious. Now it was time for her to make a personal decision. Would she reject the Messiah or accept Him? It's the same decision every individual must make when confronted with the reality of His presence. There's no middle ground when it comes to Jesus. You're either for Him or against Him. You are either saved or lost. You are either forgiven or dead in your sins.

Jesus brought this woman to a position of accepting or rejecting Him. She accepted Him and began telling others about Him.

How Jesus Sends Us

That leads to our last point. Jesus seeks us; He saves us; and He sends us. At this point in the story, the disciples returned with lunch, and they were astounded to find Jesus engaged in a conversation with a Samaritan woman of questionable morals. But the woman left her pot, went into the city, and proclaimed the news, "Come, see a Man who told me all things that I ever did. Could this be the Christ?" (verse 29)

Everyone followed her back to the well, where Jesus was waiting. Verses 39-42 says, "And many of the Samaritans of that city believed in Him because of the word of the woman who testified, 'He told me all that I ever did.' So when the Samaritans had come to Him, they urged Him to stay with them; and He stayed there two days. And many more believed because of His own word. Then they said to the woman, 'Now we believe, not because of what you said, for we ourselves have heard Him and we know that this is indeed the Christ, the Savior of the world.'"

The whole town was changed because of the conversation Jesus had that day with that woman at the well. Everyone who knows Christ as Savior has a unique story, not unlike the woman of Samaria. Jesus seeks us out and He offers us the water of life.

Jesus is the Savior of the world. He is still seeking and saving the lost, and He is sending us to reach others who are lost. He seeks us, saves us, and sends us.

1. Read John 4:1-10.

   a. Visualize the initial exchange between Jesus and the Samaritan woman in verses 7-9, as if you were directing a movie of it. What do you think the woman's first impressions were of Jesus?

   b. Jesus used a phrase in verse 10—"living water." Look up these other references to that phrase in the Bible and explain how they connect with John 4:10: Jeremiah 2:13, 17:13; John 7:38.

2. Read John 4:11-18.

   a. What did Jesus mean when He said, "Whoever drinks of the water that I shall give him will never thirst"? (verse 14)

   b. What will this water become in the one who drinks it? (verse 14)

3. Read John 4:19-26.

   a. When Jesus confronted the Samaritan woman with her immoral life in verses 17-18, how did she respond in verses 19-20?

   b. Why do you think she responded as she did?

   c. Whom did Jesus claim to be in verse 26?

4. Read John 4:27-42.

   a. How do you think the Samaritan woman responded to the Lord's invitation to follow Him and drink from the living waters?

   b. Did she ultimately believe? Why do you think she did or didn't?

GROUP QUESTIONS

1. Read John 4:1-10.

   a. We're all to share the Gospel with others, yet some people have a special giftedness in evangelism. Who do you know who is zealous and effective in soul-winning?

   b. Discuss the nature of the word "needed" in verse 4—"But He *needed* to go through Samaria" (emphasis added). Why did John choose that word?

   c. Are there ever times when you "need" to do something, but you aren't sure why or you don't really want to? How can the Lord use such occasions?

2. Read John 4:11-18.

   a. What question does the woman ask Jesus in verse 12?

   b. The Gospel of John is full of our Lord's "I AM" statements, and this would have been a perfect time for Him to say, "I am greater than Jacob." But instead, see His answer in verses 13-14. Why did He answer as He did?

3. Read John 4:19-26. Discuss the flow of conversation between Jesus and the woman.

   a. What do you think was going on in her mind?

   b. How did Jesus bring the conversation to a climactic moment?

4. Read John 4:27-42.

   a. What did the Lord mean when He said the fields are "white for harvest"?

   b. Compare John 4:35-38 with 1 Corinthians 3:6. How do we all play different roles in the evangelistic process?

DID YOU KNOW?

Samaria was a relatively small area, yet Jesus had an outsized concern for it. In John 4, He evangelized the region of Sychar, but it wasn't His only visit to Samaria. In Luke 9:51-56, He went through Samaria and encountered some hostility. In the next chapter, He told the Parable of the Good Samaritan. In Luke 17:11, He again passed through Samaria where, somewhere on His route, He healed ten lepers. In the Lord's final words to His disciples in Acts 1:8, Jesus told them be His witnesses in . . . Samaria. In Acts 8, Philip went to the capital of Samaria and preached, and there was great joy in the city. Jesus is concerned with every region, however small, and with every person on earth.

IS HE PRAYING FOR US OR ARE WE PRAYING TO HIM?

John 17

In this lesson we learn about the constant care Jesus affords His children as revealed in His great prayer for us in John 17.

OUTLINE

Although Jesus is no longer walking beside us in the physical realm, His concern for us is no less real. And the Bible tells us that one of the ways He chooses to care for us is through prayer. Being at the Father's right hand on the throne of heaven, He's also in the best place to advocate for us, to intercede for us, and to pray for us. If we want to know what He's praying, we can study His great prayer in John 17—one of the most sacred chapters in the Bible.

   I. **Jesus Is Praying for Your Security**

  II. **Jesus Is Praying for Your Sufficiency**

 III. **Jesus Is Praying for Your Maturity**

 IV. **Jesus Is Praying for Your Ministry**

  V. **Jesus Is Praying for Your Unity**

 VI. **Jesus Is Praying for Your Destiny**

Some people find it difficult to believe that Jesus cares for us in a personal way because there are so many of us. They wonder if Jesus is watching us in an impersonal way, or if He is emotionally involved with us in a way that demonstrates His compassion for our needs.

We begin to sense an answer when we notice how often Jesus expressed His care for individuals during His days on earth. He touched lepers; He cured the sick; He befriended social outcasts; He cherished children; He prayed for and forgave His murderers. Even during His agonizing death, He reassured the dying thief about Paradise. The more difficult Jesus' life became, the more He seemed to care for those around Him. When Jesus saw broken humanity, He had compassion on them.

The Bible says we can cast all our care upon Him, "for He cares for you" (1 Peter 5:7). One of the ways He cares for us is through prayer. On the final night of His earthly life, Jesus gives us a glimpse of His prayer life in John 17, which we call "Christ's High Priestly Prayer." In the first five verses, Jesus prayed for Himself. In verses 6 through 26, He prayed for His disciples and for us. Here we can learn several things about what Jesus asks when He prays for us today.

JESUS IS PRAYING FOR YOUR SECURITY

What is the one thing we pray most often for our children, especially if they're not around us? We pray for their protection and safety. In the same way, Jesus cares about our well-being and safety. He prayed in John 17, saying, "Holy Father, keep through Your name those whom You have given Me. . . . I do not pray that You should take them out of the world, but that You should keep them from the evil one" (verses 11, 15).

In these verses Jesus was asking the Father to keep us secure in the world. How we need that prayer today! We're living in dangerous times, but Jesus is praying for us. He's asking the Father to keep us safe, just as He Himself kept His disciples safe while He was on earth.

The word "keep" in verse 11 is a wonderful word, meaning "to guard or watch over." In John 6, there's a story about the disciples in the middle of the Sea of Galilee in deep trouble on a stormy night. While they were out in the boat, Jesus was up on the mountain praying. When they came to their moment of greatest trial, Jesus came to them through the storm. He had been watching over them from His place on the mountainside. Even when He wasn't in the boat with them, He was watching over them in prayer. Even when He doesn't seem near us, His eye is monitoring every event in our life.

When He prays for us, perhaps it's something like this: "Father, in the midst of their storm, in the midst of their difficulty in this world, watch over My children, protect them and keep them." He is praying for our security and safety.

We have His three-fold protection: (1) The indwelling Spirit in our heart is a garrison against the attack of the enemy; (2) the Word of God in our hands is the weapon we use for combat; (3) and in heaven overhead, like an air force, Jesus is seated at the right hand of the Father, praying for our protection. The Word of God, the Spirit of God, and the prayer of the Lord at the right hand of the Father—what powerful protection!

Psalm 121:3-8 says, "He will not allow your foot to be moved; He who keeps you will not slumber. Behold, He who keeps Israel shall neither slumber nor sleep. The Lord is your keeper; the Lord is your shade at your right hand. The sun shall not strike you by day, nor the moon by night. The Lord shall preserve you from all evil; He shall preserve your soul. The Lord shall preserve your going out and your coming in from this time forth, and even forevermore."

In John 17:15, Jesus asked the Father to protect us from the evil one. Satan is the accuser of the brethren. He goes around like a roaring lion, seeking to destroy and devour us. He wants to ruin our influence for Christ and damage our testimony. He cannot destroy our salvation, so he seeks to destroy our reputation and influence for God. He tests us and he tries to lure us into wrong decisions. But the Lord Jesus is praying that we'll not be overcome by Satan.

Jesus told Peter, "Simon, Simon! Indeed, Satan has asked for you, that he may sift you as wheat. But I have prayed for you, that your faith should not fail; and when you have returned to Me, strengthen your brethren" (Luke 22:31-32).

Jesus assured Peter he'd not face the evil one alone. He told Peter He was praying for his faith to stand. Hours later, it appeared Peter failed. He denied the Lord Jesus three times. But that wasn't the end of the story. Satan sifted him as wheat, but Jesus prayed for him, and his faith did not fail. He was restored and went on to strengthen his brothers and establish the Church on the Day of Pentecost.

We don't fully understand the spiritual warfare around us. We don't know all the ways in which the devil accuses us before God. But we have the One praying for us whose blood pleads for us. Jesus protects us from the evil one. He shields us by His prayers and by the power of His blood. His prayers are a protective force around us, and He prays for our security.

JESUS IS PRAYING FOR YOUR SUFFICIENCY

Jesus also cares about and prays for our sufficiency and for the sufficiency of our joy. In John 17:13, He prayed, "But now I come to You, and these things I speak in the world, that they may have My joy fulfilled in themselves." Jesus prayed then, and He prays now for our joy! Not just everyday joy, but overrunning joy, abundant joy, sufficient joy, fulfilled joy. This isn't the kind of happiness that depends on happenings. It's the joy that depends on Jesus.

This is related to the Hebrew word *Shalom*, which means "peace." But it means more than mere peace. It infers a sense of wellbeing, the feeling that no matter what's going on around us, we are confident and secure. This is the sufficiency and the joy of Jesus.

Jesus was a joyous person. His first miracle wasn't at a funeral but at a feast—a wedding in the town of Cana in John 2. Jesus performed many other miracles that set people on tours of rejoicing. Throughout the New Testament, He generously imparted His joy to others. One day He healed a crippled woman. She stood right up and started praising God (Luke 13:13, NIV). The Samaritan leper, healed by Jesus, returned "praising God in a loud voice" (Luke 17:15, NIV). When the lame man at the Gate Beautiful was healed, he got up and went into the temple, "walking, leaping, and praising God" (Acts 3:8).

Romans 14:17 says, "The kingdom of God is not eating and drinking, but righteousness and peace and joy in the Holy Spirit." If that's true, we ought to be the most joyous people in the world. That's why we sing triumphant, joyful psalms, hymns, and spiritual songs. Eight times in the book of Ecclesiastes, we're told to rejoice in the life that God has given us.

Lewis Smedes said, "You and I were created for joy, and if we miss it, we miss the reason for our existence!" Jesus experienced joy in His life, and right now He is praying we do the same. Our part is to say, "This is the day the Lord has made; we will rejoice and be glad in it" (Psalm 118:24). Every fresh day is a new opportunity to rejoice and say, "Today is God's gift to me, and I'm going to rejoice in it. I may not know the answers to all my problems, but I will not be defined by the difficulties of life. I will be defined by the joy of Jesus in my heart."

That is what Jesus cares about; that's what He prays for.

JESUS IS PRAYING FOR YOUR MATURITY

Jesus also cares about our maturity. In John 17:17, He prayed, "Sanctify them by Your truth. Your word is truth." The Bible is God's chief means of helping us grow into maturity. It's the food that strengthens us and causes us to grow. It provides the spiritual nutrients and emotional vitamins. It's the bread of life.

Jesus wasn't just praying that we'll learn more of the Bible, though that is important. He was praying for the Word of God to get into our life to sanctify us—to change us and mature us. As we read, study, memorize, and apply the Bible, we increasingly become more like Jesus, formed into His image to reflect His character.

JESUS IS PRAYING FOR YOUR MINISTRY

Jesus also cares about our ministries. In John 17:18, He said, "As You sent Me into the world, I also have sent them into the world." Jesus was the first missionary to planet earth. It's as if one day in heaven God called Him to the throne and said, "I need You to go to the earth where people are struggling with sin and death. You must seek and save those who are lost and pay the penalty for their sins on the cross."

In John 17, Jesus said in effect, "Just as one day You sent Me into world, now I am sending all My disciples into the world with the same message, to seek and save the lost."

That includes us! Jesus is praying for us as we carry out the mission He's given us.

Every follower of Christ has a personal ministry. We're not all ordained vocational ministers or missionaries. But we're all appointed to do the work God gives us every day. As we go about doing the ministry God has given us, we can be assured up in heaven Jesus is praying for us. He is praying for us as we preach, as we raise our children for Him, as we represent Him in our places of employment or education, as we fulfill our tasks at church, and as we seek to uplift and encourage people every day. If you have any kind of ministry, you're on His prayer list. He's praying that you would carry on to completion the work He's assigned to you.

JESUS IS PRAYING FOR YOUR UNITY

Fifth, Jesus cares about our unity. In John 17:20-21, He said, "I do not pray for these alone, but also for those who will believe in Me through their word; that they all may be one, as You, Father, are in Me, and I in You; that they also may be one in Us, that the world may believe that You sent Me."

Sometimes we hear of fighting or disagreements within a church. Few things are more vexing and unfortunate. But right now up in heaven, Jesus is praying for our unity, that we would reflect oneness according to the Bible in the same spirit that He has with the Father.

JESUS IS PRAYING FOR YOUR DESTINY

Finally, Jesus is praying for our destiny. John 17:24 says, "Father, I desire that they also whom You gave Me may be with Me where I am." We're all eager for heaven. We have so many people we miss who are already there. We look forward to the day when we'll be with Jesus and reunited with those we love. But listen to this: Jesus also wants to be with us! He wants us to be with Him where He is.

In John 14, Jesus said, "In My Father's house are many mansions; if it were not so, I would have told you. I go to prepare a place for you. And if I go and prepare a place for you, I will come again and receive you to Myself; that where I am, there you may be also" (verses 2-3).

We want to be with Him, and He wants to be with us. To be absent from the body is to be present with the Lord. As soon as we take our last breath down here, we'll take our first one up there. Christ is looking forward to that day, and it's on His prayer list that one day we will be with Him. What a destiny!

Let's review this great prayer again from John 17:

- In verses 11-12, Jesus pleads with the Father to keep us secure while we're in the world. Jesus was leaving the world and He entrusted His followers to His Heavenly Father. He asks the Father to keep us safe as He Himself had kept His disciples safe during His earthly life.

- He wants His followers to experience His joy in verse 13.
- "I do not pray that You should take them out of the world," He said in verse 15, "but that You should keep them from the evil one."
- "Sanctify them by Your truth," He said in verse 17, adding "Your word is truth."
- In verse 20, He prays for all those who will ever believe in Him, and in verse 21, He pleads that they may be one even as He is one with the Father.
- He prays for the world to recognize the true nature of our mission in verse 23.
- He also prays that we'll one day be with Him where He is so we can behold His glory "which You have given Me; for You loved Me before the foundation of the world" (verse 24).
- He ends by asking that "the love with which You loved Me may be in them, and I in them" (verse 26).

Prayer is an amazing thing. Prayer can accomplish what can never be wrought by pleading, nagging, urging, or imploring. Prayer can move people, engender healing, erode resistance, and provoke miracles. Intercessory prayer can span vast distances, enter restricted spaces, melt impenitent hearts, and solve impenetrable problems.

The Father in heaven is hearing the prayers of His Son Jesus for you right now. When He prays for us, we draw near to Him, and He draws near to us. If you don't know Him as your personal Savior, His prayer is for you to open your heart and receive Him. If you're a Christian, Jesus is praying for you along the lines of His prayer in John 17. We pray to Jesus, but Jesus is praying for us. He is interceding for us on the throne for our security, our sufficiency, our maturity, our ministry, our unity, and our destiny.

1. Read John 17:1-6.

   a. How did Jesus define eternal life in verse 3?

   b. How did Jesus bring glory to God on earth? Compare this to Paul's statement in Acts 20:24. What lesson can you learn and apply to your own life?

2. Read John 17:6-12.

   a. In verse 8, what did Jesus give His disciples?

   b. In verse 9, whom did Jesus not pray for? Whom did He pray for?

   c. In verse 11, what did Jesus ask God to do for His disciples on earth? What do you think is included in the word "keep"?

3. Read John 17:13-19.

   a. In verse 15, what does Jesus additionally pray for us? Compare this to Matthew 5:13. In light of this, how should we pray—both for ourselves and for our loved ones?

   b. According to verse 17, how does God sanctify us? What do you think is included in the word "sanctify"?

4. Read John 17:20-26.

   a. In verse 20, whom does Jesus now pray for?

   b. In verse 21, what is His great prayer request for us?

   c. In verse 24, Jesus expressed a great personal longing of His. What is it?

1. Read John 17:1-5. Compare verse 4 with Acts 20:24, Colossians 4:17, and 2 Timothy 4:7.

   a. What we can learn from these cross references?

   b. What does John 17:5 tell us about Jesus?

2. Read John 17:6-19 and discuss the following:

   a. In verse 10, how did Jesus receive glory? How can we apply the implications of that statement to our own lives?

   b. Look at verse 11. Where is Jesus going? Where are His people going to be? What does He want *for* us? What does He want *of* us?

c. In verse 13, Jesus used the words "My joy." What kind of joy does Jesus have, and what does He want to do with it?

d. Discuss how verse 15 is a powerful prayer to offer on behalf of our children, friends, missionaries, and loved ones.

e. In verse 16, Jesus said that we are "not of the world." What does that mean?

3. Read John 17:20-26.

   a. In what way does Jesus extend His prayer in verse 20? Who is now included? What does that mean to us?

   b. What is our Lord's great concern in verse 21? Why is this so difficult to achieve? How can we help bring about the answer to our Lord's request?

DID YOU KNOW?

*T*he *Jeremiah Study Bible* includes a quotation from Richard D. Phillips that sums up the intercessory ministry of Christ: "Because he lives forever, there will never be a time when this great priest cannot show forth his blood that was shed for you, when his prayers will not pour forth effectual blessing upon your life. When you die and are presented before God's throne, He will be there, pointing to the wounds he earned upon the cross, charging your debt to the account he has already paid. His priesthood is eternal, never-ending, securing eternal life to give you."

IS HE DOING GREATER WORKS OR ARE WE?

John 14:12 and Selected Scriptures

In this lesson we'll learn about our Lord's power during His earthly ministry and we'll discuss how He is doing even greater works today through His people—His Church.

OUTLINE

In reading through the Gospels, we're astounded at the supernatural power of Jesus. He performed miracles, fed multitudes, raised the dead, defied the devil, and lifted the spirits of those He met. Yet in John 14:12, He told us we would do even greater works than He did. How is that possible and what does it mean? He meant that through the Holy Spirit His people would continue to expand His work and influence. That's the stirring topic we'll tackle in this lesson.

I. **Jesus' Great Works**
   A. His Power Over Storms
   B. His Power Over Shortage
   C. His Power Over Sickness
   D. His Power Over Satan
   E. His Power Over Sadness

II. **Our Greater Works**
   A. We Have a Greater Message
   B. We Have a Greater Ministry
   C. We Can Do Greater Miracles

Many magazines and websites periodically publish lists of the most powerful or the most beautiful or the wealthiest people on the planet. But no one stays on those lists for long because life is fleeting and power is transitory. But Jesus of Nazareth possessed true beauty, wisdom, wealth, and power. Even after two thousand years, we're as gripped by the stories of His power and miracles in the Gospels as any other generation. We want to ask with His awestruck disciples, "Who can this be, that even the winds and the sea obey Him?" (Matthew 8:27)

Is it possible that we could do the kind of things He did in His infinite power, or that our deeds might exceed His? The thought would be blasphemous except for one thing—Jesus Himself said as much. In John 14:12, Jesus told His disciples, "Most assuredly, I say to you, he who believes in Me, the works that I do he will do also; and greater works than these he will do, because I go to My Father."

God makes His power available to us now. Ephesians 1:19 talks about "the exceeding greatness of His power toward us who believe." In his final known letter, Paul said, "For God has not given us a spirit of fear, but of power" (2 Timothy 1:7).

Let's look at the power Jesus exercised on earth, then we'll consider the works we can do for Him, which Jesus called "greater works than these" (John 14:12).

JESUS' GREAT WORKS

The ministry of Jesus overflows with power and powerful works. The Lord demonstrated His authority across every realm of reality, including over storms, shortages, sickness, Satan, and sadness.

His Power Over Storms

We have an example of our Lord's power over storms in Matthew 8:23-27. Jesus had been teaching throughout the day. Needing to travel across the Sea of Galilee, He got into a boat with His disciples and after launching into the water He fell asleep from fatigue. When a howling storm swamped the boat, the disciples woke Him in alarm, shouting, "Lord, save us! We are perishing!" Jesus asked them why they were so fearful, chided them for their unbelief, and then proceeded to still the storm.

Jesus knew in advance what was going to happen. He wanted to teach His disciples that no matter how great the storm, they need not worry because He is in control. When we're in a storm of our own, we have to calm ourselves enough to listen to Jesus say, "Peace, be still!" Most people are in a storm, or they've just come out of one, or they're just going into one. But the powerful One who rebuked the winds of Galilee is with us in our storms. Hallelujah! He never leaves us or forsakes us.

His Power Over Shortage

We live in a world of shortage. We don't have enough money, enough time, or enough energy. But Jesus has power over shortage. The only miracle recorded in all four Gospels (apart from the Lord's resurrection) is the feeding of the five thousand. It's likely there were more than five thousand people if you include the women and children. They had all gathered near the town of Bethsaida, a fishing village. In John's account, he mentions the Passover was near, so this happened in the springtime. The crowds followed Jesus into the hills of Galilee, and they grew hungry. Jesus asked Philip, "Where shall we buy bread, that these may eat?" The Bible says He was testing Philip, because He already knew what He was going to do. Andrew came along and said, "There is a lad here who has five barley loaves and two small fish, but what are they among so many?" (John 6:5, 9)

Jesus took the loaves and fish, looked up to heaven, and blessed them. He began breaking the food apart and distributing it to the disciples, who had organized the multitude into groups of fifty. The food kept coming and coming. It was a never-ending supply. After everyone was fed, there were twelve basketfuls left over, perhaps for each disciple to take home to his family.

John 6:6 says that Jesus knew in advance what He would do. The Lord already knows what He's going to do in all our situations as well. He has things planned in advance. Matthew 6:32 says, "For your heavenly Father knows that you need all these things." The Lord knows what we need before the need occurs and before we ask Him. When we pray, we're not giving Jesus new information. We pray because we need fellowship with Him, and He has told us to express our desires. But we can rest assured the Lord already knows all about them, and He knows how to resolve the issues that concern us.

Remember how we learned about Jesus living in the eternal present? He doesn't have to figure out what to do in the future. To Him, the future is in the present. He has power over shortage. We may not have enough money, but He knows that. We may not have enough energy; He knows that. We may not have enough space; He knows that too. He knows our needs, and He's ready to help us.

His Power Over Sickness

Jesus also exercised power over illness while on earth. He healed one person after another. Yet if we read all of the accounts, we find He didn't use any one specific method. In John 4:50, Jesus healed a nobleman's son from a distance by simply saying, "Go your way; your son lives." Miles away, the man's son suddenly recovered. On another occasion, He touched the hand of Peter's mother-in-law who was burning with fever. Her temperature returned to normal (Matthew 8:14-15).

He stretched out His hand and touched a loathsome leper, and the man's skin was healed (Mark 1:41). In Matthew 9, an ailing woman touched the hem of His garment and healing power flowed into her body and restored her health (verses 20-22).

In Matthew 9:29, Jesus touched the eyes of two blind men, and immediately they had sight. In Mark 7, He put His fingers in the ears of a deaf man, and suddenly the deaf man could hear perfectly (verses 32-35). In John 9, He spat on the ground, made clay with His saliva, and smeared it on the eyes of the blind man, telling him to go wash in the pool of Siloam. The man did so and came back seeing (verse 6-7).

In the Garden of Gethsemane, Peter swung his sword through the air and cut off the ear of the servant of the high priest. Jesus touched the man's head, and instantly his ear reattached and was perfectly restored (Luke 22:50-51).

Jesus still has power over sickness. Sometimes He heals people miraculously. Sometimes He heals us through the recuperative nature of our own bodies or through the giftedness of medical experts. But the examples of His healing in the Gospels were not exclusively for the benefit of those He healed. They were to show us His power and enable us to believe He was who He claimed to be.

One day Jesus is going to heal everyone who knows Him. All tears will be wiped away and every illness will be gone—all sorrow, crying, disease, suffering, and the ravages of aging.

All those whom Jesus healed in the Gospels eventually got sick again. They grew old and died. His temporal healing was not permanent. But our Lord's healing ministry was a token to us that one day He's going to resurrect His children in glory. We're going to have ageless bodies, and we'll realize, as we should now accept by faith, that the sufferings of this present life are not worth comparing with the glories to be revealed (Romans 8:18).

The Gospel of John devotes most of chapter 11 to the story of Jesus raising Lazarus from the dead. The Lord didn't say that Lazarus' sickness wouldn't include death. He said that it wouldn't end in death (verse 4).

Jesus arrived at Bethany after the funeral, but He stood outside of the tomb and commanded, "Lazarus, come forth!" (verse 43) The rising of Lazarus demonstrated the Lord's ultimate power over sickness and death, and it's a sign of His ability to resurrect His children from the dead and to give them incorruptible, eternal bodies fashioned like His resurrection body.

Because of the resurrection of Jesus, we can claim the promise that while we may not be healed down here, we'll all be healed up there. One day we'll have perfect bodies.

His Power Over Satan

The ministry of Jesus also demonstrated His absolute power over all the forces of evil. In particular, we can come away from the Gospels with two important facts.

1. Satan Cannot Diminish His Purity

In Matthew 4, the devil showed up in the wilderness and tempted Jesus with three different enticements. Satan was trying to derail the Gospel, spoil the plan of redemption, and get Jesus to accomplish His eternal work in a fleshly way. The Lord Jesus didn't argue with him. He just said, in effect, "Satan, it is written." Then He quoted Scripture. Interestingly, Jesus quoted from Deuteronomy, showing us that every part of Scripture is important. Satan left Him, and the angels came to minister to Him. The devil couldn't penetrate the purity of Jesus. He couldn't mar the holiness of the Son of God.

2. Spirits Cannot Defy His Authority

Throughout His ministry, Jesus was accosted by fallen spirits, or demons. They knew who He was. For example, Luke 4:33-34 says, "Now in the synagogue there was a man who had a spirit of an unclean demon. And he cried out with a loud voice, saying, 'Let us alone! What have we to do with You, Jesus of Nazareth? Did You come to destroy us? I know who You are—the Holy One of God!'"

Jesus told the demon to be quiet and to come out of the man. In a final flurry of activity, the demon came out. The watching crowd exclaimed, "What a word this is! For with authority and power He commands the unclean spirits, and they come out" (Luke 4:36).

The devil and his demons are no match against Jesus Christ. The Lord has power over them. When we feel satanic temptation going on in our lives, we must remember that Satan cannot overcome the Lord Jesus Christ. We're able to plead the blood of Christ and have victory.

His Power Over Sadness

We're all subject to sadness, and many people are sad today. We feel sadness when those we love are in trouble or when we ourselves encounter grief and hardship. We must remember that Jesus has lordship over sadness. On five occasions Jesus walked into a situation and said, "Be of good cheer."

Matthew 9:2 says, "Then behold, they brought to Him a paralytic lying on a bed. When Jesus saw their faith, He said to the paralytic, 'Son, be of good cheer; your sins are forgiven you.'" We can be cheerful because our sins have been forgiven.

When the woman crept behind Jesus and touched the hem of His robe, He turned and said to her, "Be of good cheer, daughter; your faith has made you well" (Matthew 9:22).

When the disciples were exhausted, sinking in the Sea of Galilee, Jesus came to them walking across the waves and shouting, "Be of good cheer! It is I; do not be afraid" (Matthew 14:27).

When the Twelve were distraught at the Last Supper, Jesus told them, "In the world you will have tribulation; but be of good cheer, I have overcome the world" (John 16:33).

And when the apostle Paul was imprisoned in Jerusalem, the Lord stood by him and said, "Be of good cheer, Paul; for as you have testified for Me in Jerusalem, so you must also bear witness at Rome" (Acts 23:11).

When we're glum over a situation, we can resort to these five passages and learn to be cheerful. Jesus wasn't just making a suggestion when He spoke those words. He was commanding us, "Cheer up!" What a glorious command!

We have power over our attitude through Jesus, even in the most difficult times. It's often a matter of taking a step back and seeing the situation from the perspective of eternity. God steps into our sadness with His very presence and with His words of cheer.

OUR GREATER WORKS

Jesus was a miracle-working God in all these ways, yet in John 14:12, He told Philip, "Most assuredly, I say to you, he who believes in Me, the works that I do he will do also; and greater works than these he will do, because I go to My Father."

How can we do greater works than Jesus?

When the Lord returned to heaven, He poured His Holy Spirit onto the Church as a gift from the Father. While Jesus was on earth, He was localized. Now the Holy Spirit dwells within His followers in all the nations.

We Have a Greater Message

That means we have a greater message. When Jesus was on earth, He did great things. His miracles were temporal in the physical realm. But when we present the Gospel and lead someone to Christ, a permanent and eternal change occurs. When you have eternal life, you may die physically, but you will never die spiritually. You'll always be related to God, so the greater miracle is not healing somebody from sickness. It's helping them find Jesus Christ as their personal Savior.

We Have a Greater Ministry

We also have a greater ministry. When Christ was on earth, He limited His actions to a small portion of the land. His entire ministry was done in a territory about the size of Vermont. Because He had voluntarily allowed Himself to be in the flesh, He accepted the limitations we have as humans. He could only be in one place at one time.

Once He returned to heaven, the Holy Spirit came to reside in every believer on the face of the earth. Wherever there is a Spirit-indwelt and Spirit-filled believer, ministry occurs. We can take the message of Jesus farther than He Himself took it in His own day in geographical terms. Jesus said, in essence, "When you allow Me to work in you through the Holy Spirit, greater works you will do than I did on earth, because My Father has received Me into heaven."

Martin Luther said, "[Christ] took but a little corner for Himself to preach and to work miracles in, and but a little time; whereas the apostles and their followers have spread themselves through the whole world."

Jesus told us to go into all the world and preach the Gospel, and He promised to be with us always. Through His Spirit, He is with us everywhere we go as we share the love of Jesus everywhere on earth.

We Can Do Greater Miracles

The miracles Jesus did were temporal in nature. Those who were healed by Him all later died. But when a person is healed spiritually, it's forever. That person will never die. The healing is eternal.

In the accounting system of God's Kingdom, physical and temporal results are great. But spiritual and eternal results are better. Jesus promised His disciples they would do spiritual works that would exceed His own in their geographical reach and in their eternal results.

When we tell someone about Jesus Christ and they come to Him, we can watch over the years as their life is dramatically changed. They become new people! The trajectory of their life changes— their family, their children, their grandchildren—everything is changed because of the miracle that takes place when a person gives their heart to Jesus Christ.

If our works are greater, it's because of the humble weakness of the instrument—you and me. The same power that brought regeneration and life to many, now flows through us. He came to seek and to save that which was lost. Now He lets us seek and save the lost. We can't save them in our own power, but we can point them to Jesus.

God does not call the qualified; He qualifies the called. He doesn't call us because of our résumé. He calls us because we're willing and available. He puts us in His school, and we learn how to follow Him. Then one day it dawns on us that God has called us to the greatest assignment we could ever imagine—serving Him. By every standard, this is the greatest mission in the world. Why would we stoop to do anything else? We have the greatest message, we have the greatest opportunity, and we have the greatest calling —to go into all the world.

PERSONAL QUESTIONS

1. Try to think of a handful of biblical stories about storms. Which ones frightened you the most? Why? Read Matthew 8:23-27.

   a. Jesus rebuked His disciples and He rebuked the storm. Which rebuke came first? Does that seem strange?

   b. Why do you think Jesus issued His rebukes in this order?

2. In one concise sentence, state the lesson learned from Matthew 8:23-27.

3. Read John 6:1-14. What is the primary lesson the Lord wants to teach you today from this story?

4. Review Matthew 9, and notice the various people Jesus healed and how He healed them. Why do you think the Lord used so many methods?

5. Read John 16:33 and think of one trouble or tribulation you're facing right now. If Jesus could speak to you (as He does in His Word), what would He tell you, according to this verse?

6. Read John 14:12-14.

   a. How would you explain Jesus' words in verse 12?

   b. In what way can we do even greater works than Jesus?

c. Look at verse 13. What does Jesus tell us to do? What does He promise? Why?

d. In terms of personal application, can you think of anything you're doing or any ministry with which you're involved that could be considered the "greater works" Jesus referred to in John 14:12?

e. How can you more effectively fulfill the Lord's will in this area?

f. What is one improvement you can make in serving Him?

GROUP QUESTIONS

1. Discuss the following as a group:

   a. Have you ever thought that anything you ever did was greater than what Jesus did while He was on earth?

   b. If someone told you they were doing "greater works" than Jesus, how would you react?

   c. If you had been alive in the time of Christ, observing His ministry prior to His crucifixion, what one event would have impressed you most?

2. Discuss Christ's power over storms.

   a. Can you think of other biblical stories about storms outside the Gospels?

   b. Why does God use storms to teach us lessons?

3. Read John 6:1-14.

   a. What is the significance to us of what the writer says in verse 6?

   b. How can you apply that to a situation in your life?

4. Read John 14:12-14. What is the relationship between the promise in verse 12 and the content of verses 13 and 14?

5. What works today are greater than those Jesus did while He was on earth?

6. Read John 14:15-18.

   a. Where did Jesus say the Holy Spirit would dwell?

   b. Notice the prepositions "with" and "in" in the last line of verse 17. What is their significance?

7. What do you need to do in your life now that will enable you to do the greater works of Christ?

DID YOU KNOW?

According to the *Religion News Service*, as many as fifty million people are coming to Christ each year in Africa, making it the continent with the most followers of Christ.[1] And according to a *Pew Research Center* report, by 2060, six countries with the top ten largest Christian populations will be in Africa.[2] For the last four hundred years, church growth has mostly been confined to Europe and America. But in the last few years, the growth of Christianity has exploded in Africa and Latin America, as well as in regions of Asia. Around the world, Christianity is growing faster than the population, and there are more evangelistic opportunities now than ever.

Notes

1. Wesley Granberg-Michaelson, "Where Is Christianity Headed? The View From 2019," *Religion News Service*, January 10, 2019, https://www.religionnews.com/2019/01/10/where-is-christianity-headed-the-view-from-2019.

2. Diamant, "The Countries With the 10 Largest Christian Populations and the 10 Largest Muslim Populations," *Pew Research Center*, April 1, 2019, https://www.pewresearch.org/fact-tank/2019/03/01/the-countries-with-the-10-largest-christian-populations-and-the-10-largest-muslim-populations.

Is He Living or Did He Die?

1 Corinthians 15

*In this lesson we'll study the Resurrection Chapter
of the Bible, discover the biblical facts about resurrection,
and look forward to exciting future events.*

OUTLINE

Without the reality of the resurrection—both the resurrection of
Christ on Easter Sunday and our own bodily resurrection in the
future—we have no basis for hope or optimism. We are to be pitied.
But Christ *has* risen from the dead! The Gospel is contingent on the
resurrection. In 1 Corinthians 15, Paul slowly, methodically, and
wonderfully lays out the Bible's truth regarding God's power to
resurrect us from death to life forevermore.

  I.   **The Firstfruits of the Resurrection**

 II.   **The Foundation of the Resurrection**

III.   **The Future Order of the Resurrection**
       A. Stage One: The Resurrection of Jesus Christ
       B. Stage Two: The Resurrection of the Saved
       C. Stage Three: The Resurrection of the Unbelievers

IV.   **The Final Result of the Resurrection**
       A. Jesus Will Deliver the Kingdom
       B. Jesus Will Destroy Death

The reality of the life, death, and resurrection of Jesus Christ is the centerpiece of world history and the core of Christian belief. It was anticipated throughout the Old Testament, described in the Gospels, proclaimed in the book of Acts, and explained in the New Testament epistles. There is one special chapter of the Bible that devotes a full 58 unbroken verses to pressing home the significance of the bodily resurrection of Jesus Christ. We call this the Resurrection Chapter of the Bible—1 Corinthians 15. If you were to compile the fifteen most important chapters in the Bible, this one should be on your list.

Apparently there were some people in the Corinthian church who were confused about the resurrection. They didn't quite understand the reality or the nature of Christ's bodily resurrection from the dead, and they didn't have a firm grasp on their theology or doctrine about the future resurrection of believers. Paul takes his time and explains in detail the entire reality, concept, sequence, and nature of God's plan regarding the resurrection of the body.

The chapter opens with a clear and concise definition of the Gospel: "Christ died for our sins according to the Scriptures, and that He was buried, and that He rose again the third day according to the Scriptures" (verses 3-4). These are the facts of the Gospel—the Good News. Paul insisted the resurrection of Christ be part of that definition, and we must insist on it being a pivotal part of our life. Paul goes on to say that if the resurrection is a fraud, "we are of all men the most pitiable" (verse 19). But, he says, Christ *has been raised* from the dead (verse 20)!

THE FIRSTFRUITS OF THE RESURRECTION

Hallelujah! The resurrection of Jesus Christ is not in question nor in doubt. We rejoice to know Christ is risen—and to know the risen Christ on a personal basis. But there is something more to bear in mind: Jesus' resurrection was not just about Him. It's about us too. First Corinthians 15:20 says, "But now Christ is risen from the dead, and has become the firstfruits of those who have fallen asleep."

The word *firstfruits* goes back to Leviticus 23, when the Lord established a series of annual holy days for the nation of Israel. There were seven major festivals or feasts. The third was the Feast of Firstfruits, which is a word referring to the earliest crops of the harvest season. God told the Israelites, "When you come into the land which I give to you, and reap its harvest, then you shall bring a sheaf of the firstfruits of your harvest to the priest. He shall wave the sheaf before the Lord, to be accepted on your behalf; on the day after the Sabbath the priest shall wave it" (verses 10-11).

In other words, on the first day of this feast a person would be selected to go out and mark a spot in the grain fields where a sheath would be cut. On the second day of the feast, the sheath would be cut and brought into the sanctuary. On the third day, the sheath would be presented to the Lord as a symbol that the rest of the harvest would later be gathered and that a tithe of that harvest would be given back to God. The firstfruits were presented on the first day of the week, which coincides with the day of Christ's resurrection.

The firstfruits were a symbol that the first of the grain had been harvested, but there would be more to come—much more. Jesus was the firstfruits of the resurrection, indicating that the full resurrection harvest is still to come. If we die before Jesus comes back, our body will go into the grave, but our spirit and soul will go to be with the Lord. One day our body will be raised up just as the Lord Jesus was two thousand years ago. His resurrection is the guarantee and the promise that there are more resurrections to come.

This isn't just a message for Easter Sunday. It's a living reality for us every moment of every day. Christ is alive! And because He lives, we will live also. Romans 8:11 says, "But if the Spirit of Him who raised Jesus from the dead dwells in you, He who raised Christ from the dead will also give life to your mortal bodies through His Spirit who dwells in you." The tinge of this glorious truth should touch every thought, every conversation, and every sermon. It should brighten every day.

THE FOUNDATION OF THE RESURRECTION

The passage in 1 Corinthians 15 goes on to say: "For since by man came death, by Man also came the resurrection of the dead. For as in Adam all die, even so in Christ all shall be made alive" (verses 21-22).

According to verse 21, the tragedy of sin and death came into this world through one man—Adam. Before Adam sinned there was no death. But when he disobeyed God, a separation occurred and death came upon humanity. But in this verse Paul says another Man came into the world, and He has the power to reverse the death sentence of Adam and give us resurrection victory and eternal life. That second Man is Christ. Through one man came death; through another Man came life.

We have two different categories of humanity—Adam's race and Jesus' race—the race of natural man and the race of spiritual Man. Adam is the federal head of the natural race. Because he sinned, we've inherited his DNA of death. We're all in Adam's race. But when we come to Christ, we enter His race and have part in His resurrection.

There's never a day when those in Christ are separated from the presence of our living Lord. When we receive Him as Savior, we pass from the hopelessness of Adam to the certain hope of Christ.

THE FUTURE ORDER OF THE RESURRECTION

Paul's Resurrection Chapter continues in verse 23 to explain the order of the resurrection: "But each one in his own order: Christ the firstfruits, afterward those who are Christ's at His coming." In the Bible, resurrection is a preeminent theme. We have the resurrection of Christ, but there are other resurrections yet to come.

Stage One: The Resurrection of Jesus Christ

Stage one is the resurrection of Jesus Christ. He was the first Person resurrected—the firstfruits. That doesn't mean He was the first dead person to be raised back to life. There were other people in the Old Testament and in the Gospels who were raised from the dead, like the son of the widow of Zarephath in 1 Kings 17 and Jairus' daughter in Mark 5. But the resurrection of Jesus was qualitatively different from any other. All the other people who were raised eventually grew old or sick, and they died again. They were not permanently, eternally, gloriously resurrected. They were simply raised from the dead.

When Jesus rose on the Sunday morning following His crucifixion, His body was resurrected in power and glory, never again to age, grow sick, or die. He was physically equipped for everlasting life. He is the first resurrection—the firstfruits. This is a wonderful fact for all of us. When we get to know the resurrected Jesus, we're getting to know Jesus as He is today.

Stage Two: The Resurrection of the Saved

The next event in God's schedule of resurrections will be the resurrection of believers, and this will happen in two phases.

1. At the Rapture

Currently we're living in the Church Age, the age of grace. It began on the Day of Pentecost in Acts 2, and it will continue until Jesus comes for His Church when we'll be resurrected and raptured—caught up to be with Him. The Bible says, "For the Lord Himself will descend from heaven with a shout, with the voice of an archangel, and with the trumpet of God. And the dead in Christ will rise first" (1 Thessalonians 4:16). This is the next resurrection on the horizon—all who have died in Christ during the Church Age. As we are being resurrected, the Lord will clothe us with new resurrected bodies. Philippians 3:21 says, "[Christ] will transform our lowly body that it may be conformed to His glorious body."

The apostle John said it this way: "We know that when He is revealed, we shall be like Him, for we shall see Him as He is" (1 John 3:2).

2. At the End of the Tribulation

The next resurrection will occur approximately seven years after the Rapture. The event of the Rapture, which is explained in 1 Thessalonians 4, will help trigger a seven-year period of great difficulty on earth. It's the Tribulation, which is described in Revelation 6–18. During this seven-year period, 144,000 Jewish evangelists will be preaching the Gospel around the globe. Two special witnesses will be preaching in downtown Jerusalem. Multitudes will turn from the horror they see coming on the earth, and they will be saved by the message of the Gospel. This will be the greatest spiritual awakening in world history. Hundreds of thousands of people will be saved during the Tribulation period, and many of those will pay for their salvation with their life. They will be martyred. The Antichrist and his forces will seek to destroy every one of these converts. At the end of the Tribulation, there will be another resurrection.

Revelation 20:4 says, "Then I saw the souls of those who had been beheaded for their witness to Jesus and for the word of God, who had not worshiped the beast or his image, and had not received his mark on their foreheads or on their hands. And they lived."

Daniel 12:1-2 says, "At that time Michael shall stand up, the great prince who stands watch over the sons of your people; and there shall be a time of trouble, such as never was since there was a nation, even to that time. And at that time your people shall be delivered, every one who is found written in the book. And many of those who sleep in the dust of the earth shall awake, some to everlasting life, some to shame and everlasting contempt."

When Christ returns to reign during the Millennium, not a single believer's body from Adam until that very moment will remain in the grave. All of those who have been saved during the Church Age will have gone up and been resurrected at the Rapture. All of those who died in the Tribulation, as well as all of the Old Testament saints, will be resurrected at the end of the Tribulation.

Stage Three: The Resurrection of the Unbelievers

To review, we live in the Church Age, but Jesus may come at any moment to rapture and resurrect His Church. Following this Rapture, the world will descend into seven years of tribulation, and at the end of that period the Lord will come back to earth, and all the Great Tribulation martyrs and Old Testament saints will be raised. They will reign with Jesus for a thousand years, which is what we call the Millennium. Jesus will be King of kings and Lord of lords on this earth. He will reign in righteousness and peace.

The final resurrection will come at the end of the Millennial Reign of Christ. All the unsaved, all the lost, all those who have rejected Christ—they will be resurrected and will stand before God at the Great White Throne Judgment. Revelation 20:12-13 says, "And I saw the dead, small and great, standing before God, and books were opened. And another book was opened, which is the Book of Life. And the dead were judged according to their works, by the things which were written in the books. The sea gave up the dead who were in it, and Death and Hades delivered up the dead who were in them. And they were judged, each one according to his works."

There will be no saved people at the Great White Throne Judgment. All who stand before God at that awful moment will be condemned and sent to hell because of their rejection of Jesus Christ.

THE FINAL RESULT OF THE RESURRECTION

As we come to the last part of this passage, we learn there will be two final results of the series of resurrections we've described.

Jesus Will Deliver the Kingdom

First, Jesus Christ is going to deliver the kingdom to God the Father. First Corinthians 15:24-25 says, "Then comes the end, when He delivers the kingdom to God the Father, when He puts an end to all rule and all authority and power. For He must reign till He has put all enemies under His feet."

A day is coming when the desire for a perfect world will be fully accomplished. His kingdom will come, and that worldwide kingdom will not fail, as all human kingdoms do, for it will be ruled by the perfect Son of God—the resurrected Christ.

Jesus didn't come into this world just to redeem us; He came to redeem the whole universe. Romans 8:22 says that the entire cosmos is groaning in expectation of the day when God will set it free from the curse and fully redeem it. One day there will be a great renovation of this world and of the whole universe. Revelation 21:1 says, "Now I saw a new heaven and a new earth, for the first heaven and the first earth had passed away."

After the resurrections, Jesus will have finished His ultimate work of redemption, and we'll live in the kind of paradise we so deeply crave in our heart.

Jesus Will Destroy Death

Furthermore, there will be no more death—ever! The next verse in 1 Corinthians 15 says, "The last enemy that will be destroyed is death" (verse 26). And there's one final verse in this paragraph—verse 28: "Now when all things are made subject to Him, then the Son Himself will also be subject to Him who put all things under Him, that God may be all in all."

Jesus will deliver all His work to the Father, and the Father will glorify the Son, and He will reign forever and ever.

Right now, most of us are more preoccupied with death than we realize. We worry about our aches, pangs, twinges, and doctors' appointments. And we worry about our children and loved ones when they travel or have any kind of medical emergency. Some people go through life terrified by the thought of death. The book of Hebrews speaks of those who are held in the grip of bondage all their lives because of their fear of death. But one day our resurrected King will wrap the chains of eternity and the strength of His glorious power around death, and He will throw death into the Lake of Fire. Death will be gone, and we'll never have to face it again.

The Bible says in heaven there will be no more dying!

Jesus Christ is alive today. He's at the right hand of the Father, and one day He's coming back. Scour the religions of our day and you'll see that none of them have a living leader. But when we accept Jesus Christ, we meet a living Savior. He forgives us for everything we've ever done or will do. He takes away the guilt and replaces it with peace and with the sense of His presence in our life.

Why would we not want to make that important decision today, to put our trust in Him? We can do that by coming in full sincerity and confessing our sins, proclaiming Christ as Lord.

PERSONAL QUESTIONS

1. Read 1 Corinthians 15:1-4. Here Paul describes the Gospel in its essence. What are the basic facts he lays out?

2. Read 1 Corinthians 15:5-11.

   a. To whom did Jesus appear after His death and resurrection?

   b. The list Paul gives here is not complete, for we know of other resurrection appearances in the Gospels. But this is important. Do any of those names or groups strike you as especially significant?

3. Read 1 Corinthians 15:12-18.

   a. What would be true if the body of Jesus Christ had never returned to life?

   b. What would it mean for us to have a dead Savior?

4. Study 1 Corinthians 15:20. Based on this lesson, what is the significance of the word *firstfruits*?

5. According to 1 Corinthians 15:21-22, what is the difference between Adam and Jesus?

6. Read 1 Corinthians 15:23-28. What are some of the events that will occur in the future?

7. Read 1 Corinthians 15:51-57. Now read 1 Thessalonians 4:13-18. As you read these verses, what single fact thrills you the most?

8. Read the final verse of the chapter—1 Corinthians 15:58. Because of the coming resurrection, what should you be doing now?

GROUP QUESTIONS

1. As a group, discuss whether Christianity is a viable religion or faith-system without the reality of the bodily resurrection of Jesus Christ. Could Christianity survive without the literal resurrection of the Lord?

2. Read 1 Corinthians 15:1-11. Paul begins his Resurrection Chapter by discussing the facts. As a group discuss the following questions:

   a. What is the essence of the Gospel?

   b. Who were the eyewitnesses?

3. Discuss a world where there was no resurrection, no Easter.

   a. What would that be like?

   b. How would our world be different today?

   c. How would you be different? (See 1 Corinthians 15:12-19.)

4. According to 1 Corinthians 15:20, discuss the significance of the word *firstfruits*. (See also Leviticus 23:9-14.)

5. In what ways are Adam and Christ alike? In what ways are they different? (See 1 Corinthians 15:21-23.)

6. Based upon verses 23-28, make a simple list of the activities that will occur in the future. This is a succinct prophecy about the great coming epochs in earth's future. Can you think of other Scriptures that amplify some of these points?

7. According to verses 51-57, in what way will our body be changed at the coming resurrection?

8. Read the last verse of the chapter—1 Corinthians 15:58. In view of these glorious coming events, what should we be doing now?

Besides the Lord Jesus, eight specific people were raised to life in the Bible—three in the Old Testament, three in the Gospels, and two in Acts. The son of the widow of Zarephath was raised back to life by Elijah in 1 Kings 17. Elisha raised the son of the Shunammite woman in 2 Kings 4. After Elisha died, a man was placed in his tomb, who was instantly raised in 2 Kings 13 when he touched Elisha's bones (verses 20-21). Jesus Himself raised three people to life—the son of the widow of Nain in Luke 7; the daughter of Jairus in Mark 5, and Lazarus in John 11. Peter raised Dorcas to life in Acts 9, and Paul raised up Eutychus in Acts 20.

IS HE PAST OR
IS HE PRESENT?

Selected Scriptures

In this lesson, we'll learn the seven ways Jesus described Himself using the "I AM" formula highlighted in the Gospel of John—and we'll learn what these titles mean to us.

OUTLINE

Jesus is indescribable because there is no precedent for Him. He is unique in history. But to help us understand His various roles on earth, He used a series of statements recorded by John in the Fourth Gospel—the "I AM" statements of Jesus. By employing a set of everyday images like bread, light, and vines, Jesus made some of His most profound truths simple enough for us to visualize and understand. Our study will survey the seven "I AM" statements of Christ in John's Gospel.

   I.   **I Am the Bread of Life**

  II.   **I Am the Light of the World**

 III.   **I Am the Door**

 IV.   **I Am the Good Shepherd**
      A. The Good Shepherd Loves His Sheep
      B. The Good Shepherd Leads His Sheep
      C. The Good Shepherd Lays Down His Life for His Sheep

  V.   **I Am the Resurrection and the Life**

 VI.   **I Am the Way, the Truth, and the Life**

 VII.   **I Am the True Vine**

There are statues of Jesus all around the world, countless paintings of Him in museums, and crosses and crucifixes in almost every church. But the statues, pictures, symbols, and images have no power in themselves. What we need is the true and living Christ within us and among us. We have trouble describing Him because He is indescribable. How do you explain God? And how do you describe the miracle of God becoming a man? But Jesus had no trouble describing Himself. He used the phrase "I AM," which was an Old Testament phrase employed as a title for God. It comes from Exodus 3, when the Lord said to Moses, "I AM WHO I AM" (verse 14). That phrase speaks of God's self-existence. He is the ever-present One. He didn't say, "I WAS" or "I WILL BE." He is "I AM."

Jesus took that phrase and applied it to Himself repeatedly in the Gospel of John. On one occasion, He infuriated His critics by saying, "Most assuredly, I say to you, before Abraham was, I AM" (John 8:58). Abraham had been gone for two thousand years, yet Jesus claimed to predate him.

Using that phrase, Jesus developed a series of statements that are pictures and images of His Person and work. On seven different occasions in John's Gospel, He said, "I am," going on to list another title, figure, and metaphor. He said of himself: "I am the Bread of Life, the Light of the World, the Door, the Good Shepherd, the Resurrection and Life, the Way, the Truth, and the Life, and the True Vine."

I AM THE BREAD OF LIFE

In John 6:35, Jesus said, "I am the bread of life." This statement comes in the same chapter in which Jesus fed the five thousand men with the little boy's lunch. Taking two fish and five loaves of bread, Jesus broke and multiplied them until He had fed a crowd that numbered at least fifteen thousand, when counting the women and children. The crowd was thrilled to get a free lunch, and perhaps some of them thought about the manna God provided for the Israelites in the wilderness. They wondered if Jesus was the new Moses who had come to provide food for them every day.

Back in the synagogue of Capernaum, Jesus said, "Most assuredly, I say to you, Moses did not give you the bread from heaven, but My Father gives you the true bread from heaven. For the bread of God is He who comes down from heaven and gives life to the world" (John 6:32-33).

It wasn't Moses who gave them bread from heaven, Jesus explained. It was God. And the manna didn't last long. It spoiled after one day. Jesus is far better. He is the eternal Bread of God. His listeners still didn't understand, and they said, "Lord, give us this bread always" (John 6:34). They apparently thought Jesus was going to give them fish and loaves every day. So Jesus sought to explain He wasn't speaking about literal bread. He said, "I am the bread of life. He who comes to Me shall never hunger, and he who believes in Me shall never thirst" (John 6:35).

As the Bread of Life, Jesus is to our spiritual being what physical bread is to our physical being. He is the core sustenance for our inner being. He meets our needs, satisfies our appetite for fulfillment and eternal life, and is a daily blessing to us. Jesus is our bread.

I AM THE LIGHT OF THE WORLD

In the genius of John's unfolding Gospel, the One who said, "I am the bread of life" next calls Himself the Light of the World. In John 8:12, Jesus said, "I am the light of the world. He who follows Me shall not walk in darkness, but have the light of life."

These words were spoken in the context of the woman taken in adultery at the first part of the eighth chapter of John. A crowd dragged this woman to Jesus because she had committed immorality. They wanted to see what Jesus would do. They were testing Him. They wanted to hear what He would say. But Jesus didn't say anything. Instead, He stooped down and wrote something in the dirt.

Then Jesus told the crowd that whoever was without sin should cast the first stone. One by one, the people turned and left; He told the woman to go on her way too and to give up her life of immorality. Shortly afterward, Jesus went on to say, "I am the light of the world. He who follows Me shall not walk in darkness, but have the light of life" (verse 12).

He had just told this woman, "Go and sin no more" (verse 11). But He made it clear that we can all stay out of darkness by walking in the light that radiates from Him.

In the next chapter, Jesus repeated Himself. This time His words were spoken within the context of a man who had been blind from birth. This man had never seen light, and Jesus said, "As long as I am in the world, I am the light of the world" (John 9:5).

On yet another occasion, Jesus used the phrase, "the light of the world." This time, however, He wasn't talking about Himself —but us. In Matthew 5:14-16, He said, "You are the light of the world. A city that is set on a hill cannot be hidden. Nor do they light a lamp and put it under a basket, but on a lampstand, and it gives light to all who are in the house. Let your light so shine before men, that they may see your good works and glorify your Father in heaven."

God wants us to be spiritual lights in a dark world. In essence, He was saying something like this: "As long as I am in this world, I am the light. But when I return to heaven, you are going to be lights in the darkness on My behalf."

It's as though He is the sun and we are the moon. We can't generate light, but we can reflect it. We have no light in ourselves. We are reflectors. The only way we can shine brighter is by keeping our reflectors clean. We have to use the cleansing agent of Scripture to keep our lives morally pure and emotionally healthy. We want to influence our society for the Lord and make a difference in our culture. That's why we do good works and help others in Jesus' name.

I AM THE DOOR

We find our Lord's next "I AM" statement in John 10:7-10: "Most assuredly, I say to you, I am the door of the sheep. All who ever came before Me are thieves and robbers, but the sheep did not hear them. I am the door. If anyone enters by Me, he will be saved, and will go in and out and find pasture. The thief does not come except to steal, and to kill, and to destroy. I have come that they may have life, and that they may have it more abundantly."

In the days of Christ, people would shepherd their sheep out in the fields until it was time to come home to the corral or fold— the fenced-in area where the sheep could be safe or spend the night. The fold was a stone structure with the opening for a door in one section, but there was no door attached. Instead, the shepherd himself would stretch out lengthwise in the doorway and make his bed there. Nothing could threaten the sheep without coming across the shepherd.

Jesus said, "I am the door." In other words, if you're one of the sheep who belongs to Jesus, you have to climb over His body to get in and you would have to climb over His body to get out. You belong to Him; He knows your name. He is the Door to the sheepfold. Thieves and robbers try to come in over the walls, but we can only get in through the Door—Jesus Himself.

I AM THE GOOD SHEPHERD

In the same chapter and passage, Jesus referred to Himself as the Good Shepherd. In John 10:11, He said, "I am the good shepherd." He repeated this in verse 14, saying, "I know My sheep, and am known by My own." This image became a favorite drawing in the catacombs among the early Christians. It's been a special biblical picture from the earliest pages of the Bible. Jesus was undoubtedly thinking here of Psalm 23, when He identified Himself as the Shepherd. Jesus never referred to Himself as a priest. He never referred to Himself as a preacher or a clergyman. He never said He was a bishop or an elder. But He was happy to call Himself the Good Shepherd. There are many implications to this figure of speech. Let's zero in on three of them.

The Good Shepherd Loves His Sheep

In biblical days, shepherds became emotionally attached to their sheep, and the sheep to their shepherd. It shouldn't surprise us because many people have a pet with whom they become close. Think of how much time the sheep and the shepherd spent together, often in lonely places. The shepherds gave each sheep a name, just as we name our pets today. They called their sheep by name, and when the animals came into the fold they were counted to make sure none of them had strayed away.

Sheep are totally helpless without a shepherd. In the same way, we are as helpless in our Christian walk in the world as sheep without a shepherd. We need a Shepherd, One who calls us by name. We need a Shepherd who knows us. We need a Shepherd who makes sure we get in the fold before dark and who protects us from beasts and thieves.

The Good Shepherd Leads His Sheep

Sometimes life feels like a map with the names of all the roads, streets, towns, and cities missing. It's just a bunch of lines, and we have no idea where to go or how to get there. The future can be complicated, and decision making is difficult. But we can pray, "Lord, I don't know what to do, but my eyes are on You."

How do we find God's will? The way to know the will of God is to stay close to the Shepherd. Keep a tight relationship with Him. He has the way all mapped out, and as long as we stay close to Him, we will always be in the will of God. For the will of God is found in the process of walking with the Shepherd, staying close to Him.

Psalm 32:8 says, "I will instruct you and teach you in the way you should go; I will guide you with My eye."

Isaiah 30:21 says, "Your ears shall hear a word behind you, saying, 'This is the way, walk in it,' whenever you turn to the right hand or whenever you turn to the left."

The Good Shepherd Lays Down His Life for His Sheep

The Good Shepherd not only loves us and leads us, but He has laid down His life for us. The writers of the Bible didn't have highlighters or other ways to emphasize a point, so they repeated the point over and over when they felt it was unusually important. Jesus did this in John 10, saying, "I am the good shepherd. The good shepherd gives His life for the sheep. . . . I lay down My life for the sheep. . . . I lay down My life that I may take it again . . . I lay it down of Myself. I have power to lay it down" (verses 11, 15, 17, 18).

How would you answer the question, "Who killed Jesus?" Was it the Romans? Jewish leaders? You and me with our sins? In some way, all of those are true; but Jesus said no one took His life from Him. He laid it down on His own. Our Lord's death was voluntary. He spoke of laying it down and taking it back up. No one took His life from Him, for no one had the authority to do so. The Good Shepherd, the Son of God, voluntarily, willingly of His own volition, out of love, laid down His life for you and for me. He did so to provide us with the forgiveness of sins and everlasting life.

I AM THE RESURRECTION AND THE LIFE

Our Lord's next "I AM" statement is in John 11, where He calls Himself the Resurrection and the Life. In this chapter, Jesus hears that His friend Lazarus was ill, but Jesus delayed going to see him.

By the time He arrived, the funeral had already taken place. The man's sisters, Mary and Martha, were understandably distraught.

Martha met Him before He arrived and said, "Lord, if You had been here, my brother would not have died. But even now I know that whatever You ask of God, God will give You" (verses 21-22).

That's when Jesus uttered these incredible words: "I am the resurrection and the life. He who believes in Me, though he may die, he shall live. And whoever lives and believes in Me shall never die. Do you believe this?" (John 11:25-26)

Many of the Jewish people of our Lord's day did not believe Him, and the sect called the Sadducees didn't even believe there was any such hope as a resurrection. Yet Jesus called Himself the "resurrection." He claimed to be the very personification of the reality of resurrection and life.

Jesus is not just the I AM for now, He's the I AM for the future. We die, and our body turns to dust and ashes. But the same Jesus who created us the first time knows how to reconstruct and resurrect us. The scattered remnants of our old body will be reconstituted into a new, glorified body prepared for eternity. Philippians 3:20-21 says: "But our citizenship is in heaven. And we eagerly await a Savior from there, the Lord Jesus Christ, who, by the power that enables him to bring everything under his control, will transform our lowly bodies so that they will be like his glorious body" (NIV).

I AM THE WAY, THE TRUTH, AND THE LIFE

Our study continues into John 14, where Jesus said something our culture today finds very offensive: "I am the way, the truth, and the life. No one comes to the Father except through Me" (John 14:6). One of the biggest issues today is the Gospel's claim to be the exclusive way to have a relationship with God. People think there are many ways to God, and assert that the important thing is not what we believe but our sincerity in believing it.

In order to get to heaven, we have to be born again, and there's only one way for that to happen. It's through Christ Jesus. He is the Way, the Truth, and the Life—and the only way.

I AM THE TRUE VINE

The Lord's final "I AM" statement is in John 15: "I am the true vine, and My Father is the vinedresser. . . . Abide in Me, and I in you. As the branch cannot bear fruit of itself, unless it abides in the vine, neither can you, unless you abide in Me" (verses 1-4).

When we study this topic in this chapter, we can't help but notice there is a progression in this passage about fruitfulness. Jesus said in verse 2: "Every branch that bears fruit He prunes, that it may bear more fruit." And in verse 8 He said, "By this My Father is glorified, that you bear much fruit; so you will be My disciples."

We're to bear fruit (verse 2), more fruit (verse 2), and much fruit (verses 5 and 8).

We have to stay connected to the Lord, just like a vine is connected to a branch. And sometimes the Gardener—God the Father—prunes us. That is, He removes things from our lives—He prunes us—so we'll be more productive. He knows what's most important, and He knows what needs to be removed from our life. He does it all so we'll be as productive for Him as possible.

We all have to ask ourselves these questions about Jesus: Is He my Bread of Life? Is He my Light of the World? Is He my Door? My Shepherd? My Way and Truth and Life? Is He my True Vine and am I firmly attached to Him and bearing much fruit?

PERSONAL QUESTIONS

1. If someone asked you to suggest a metaphor or symbol for your life, how would you answer? In other words, finish this sentence: "I am . . ."

2. Read John 6:32-35.

   a. Do you enjoy bread? If so, why do you think that is true?

   b. In what way is Jesus like manna or bread for your life?

   c. How can you apply this truth to your life today?

3. Read John 8:12 and 9:5. Name some of the ways in which Jesus is like light.

4. Read John 10:1-18.

   a. In what way does this passage remind you of Psalm 23?

   b. Name two or three ways in which Jesus is like a shepherd to you.

5. Read John 11:20-26.

   a. Do you sense Martha's hurt or frustration? In her humanity, was it justified?

   b. How do you think Jesus' words comforted her?

   c. What comfort do they offer us today?

6. Read John 14:1-6. These are some of the most comforting words in the Bible, yet they are among the most controversial.

   a. Why does the world reject the claim of Jesus in verse 6?

   b. Why must a person accept this truth in order to be a Christian?

7. Read John 15:1-8. Jesus is speaking of grapevines, but many plants have a main trunk and connected branches.

   a. What causes a vine or fruit tree to be productive?

   b. Is there one certain way in which you could be more closely connected to the branch—to Jesus?

GROUP QUESTIONS

1. Read John 6:32-35 together as a group. As simple as it is, some people have difficulty understanding what Jesus meant when He said, "I am the bread of life."

   a. Take turns discussing what it means for Him to be the Bread of Life in today's world.

   b. As a group consider and discuss how Jesus is nourishment to each of you personally.

2. Read John 8:12 and Matthew 5:14-16. Jesus specifically pointed out that good deeds are the way we can shine our light on the world. What are some deeds you can do personally or as a group to shine the light of God's love to others?

3. Read John 10:7-10 and discuss the cultural insights that were given this lesson. In your own experience, in what way is Jesus serving as the Door for you?

4. Read John 10:11-14.

   a. In what way is this passage similar to Psalm 23?

   b. Discuss this following: When you think of the Lord as your Shepherd, what brings you the most comfort?

5. Read John 11:21-26.

   a. Do you think Mary and Martha frequently looked out the window or walked down the lane looking for Jesus as their brother was dying?

   b. Has there ever been a time when Jesus delayed in answering a need in your own life?

   c. If comfortable, share with the group the lesson you learned while you waited on the Lord.

6. As a group read John 14:1-6. How would you answer a critic who rejects the exclusive nature of the Gospel? Discuss.

7. Read John 15:1-8 together as group. Discuss the lessons that this remarkable analogy speaks most clearly to each of you.

DID YOU KNOW?

Bread in its many forms is among the most widely consumed food in the world. It's portable, compact, and it can be healthy if made in the right way from the right ingredients. The earliest bread was made from grain ground by hand with rocks, reportedly in Egypt. The Mesopotamians refined the process by inventing milling stones during Old Testament days. Until the early 1900s, all bread was sliced by hand until Otto Rohwedder created the first mechanized bread slicer. Within a decade, ninety percent of store-bought bread was then sliced by machine.

IS HE KING OF THE JEWS OR KING OF KINGS?

Selected Scriptures

In this lesson we study the royal titles of Jesus—His kingly titles—and what it means to us today that Jesus is seated on His heavenly throne.

OUTLINE

The entire Bible is about Jesus Christ, and within its pages we find scores of names and titles for Him—Immanuel, Son of God, Son of Man, Alpha and Omega, the Good Shepherd, Messiah, and so many others. All of these titles show us various facets of His life and work. One category of titles are exclusively royal—His kingship titles. He reigns as King in various realms, and as we'll discover in this lesson, each of His royal titles brings a unique blessing to our life.

I.   **His Royal Titles**
    A. King of the Jews
    B. King of Israel
    C. King of Kings
    D. King Over All the Earth
    E. King of Glory

II. **His Regal Throne**
    A. Praise Him With All Your Heart
    B. Bring Him All Your Needs
    C. Trust Him in All Your Circumstances
    D. Anticipate Him Through All Your Days

Among the historic figures that have dotted the landscape of history, few have been called "Great." These characters are like monuments on the pages of time; they are rulers who wielded extraordinary power or left an unusual mark. In the time of the Bible we have Cyrus the Great, Darius the Great, Xerxes the Great, and Herod the Great. Between the Old and New Testaments, the world was changed forever by the rise of Alexander the Great. Europe later came under the sway of Charles the Great.

Encyclopedias list more than 130 characters in history known as "the Great." But the greatest King the world has ever known is Jesus, and He is never referred to in the Bible as "Jesus the Great." His greatness isn't derived from a comparison with other people. He is in a class by Himself. He stands absolutely alone in history, for He is Jesus Christ, the King of kings and the Lord of lords.

He is the King whose power is absolute, whose reign is infinite, whose throne is unconquerable. He's an indescribable King, for He eternally reigns without the beginning of days or ending of life. He was born a King and He died a King. Revelation 1:5 refers to Him as, "Jesus Christ, the faithful witness, the firstborn from the dead, and the ruler over the kings of the earth."

HIS ROYAL TITLES

He's our Messiah; He's our Intercessor, the Compassionate Servant, the Humble Teacher, the Selfless Savior. But never forget, along with all those relational terms, He is the King. Without His supreme and sovereign rule, our life would sink into chaos. Nothing can stabilize our emotions like remembering His royal reign. He commands and He controls, and nothing is exempt from His preeminent power. That's why so many people find Him the anchor of their souls. He is the King of kings. He is the Lord of lords, He's the Sovereign of all the earth.

King of the Jews

There are two periods in His life when Jesus was referred to as the King of the Jews. Matthew 2:1-2 says, "Now after Jesus was born in Bethlehem of Judea in the days of Herod the king, behold, wise men from the East came to Jerusalem, saying, 'Where is He who has been born King of the Jews?'" Local rabbis told them of

Micah's prophecy about Bethlehem as the birthplace of Christ, and so the Magi traveled on to Bethlehem. The narrative continues in verse 11: "And when they had come into the house, they saw the young Child with Mary His mother, and fell down and worshiped Him. And when they had opened their treasures, they presented gifts to Him: gold, frankincense, and myrrh."

We've all seen a thousand Christmas cards of this scene, but try to picture it in your mind. These were strange visitors from eastern lands, bowing down in regal robes, excitedly offering gifts and worshiping Jesus as the King of the Jews. Even in His infancy, Jesus was a King. Others become kings upon the death of another, but Jesus was born a King that He might die for another—for you and for me.

That leads us to His death, where He is also referred to as the King of the Jews. Almost without exception, there's no mention of this title between His birth and His death, but it wasn't forgotten. When Jesus stood before the Roman Governor Pontius Pilate at His trial, the man asked Him, "Are You the King of the Jews?" Jesus replied, "It is as you say" (Matthew 27:11).

Mark 15:9-12 says, "Pilate answered them, saying, 'Do you want me to release to you the King of the Jews?' For he knew that the chief priests had handed Him over because of envy. But the chief priests stirred up the crowd, so that he should rather release Barabbas to them. Pilate answered and said to them again, 'What then do you want me to do with Him whom you call the King of the Jews?'"

They responded in verse 13 by crying out, "Crucify Him!"

When Jesus was nailed to the cross, a sign was placed above His head, reading "THE KING OF THE JEWS" (Mark 15:26). The chief priest and Jewish leaders objected, but Pilate refused to change the wording (John 19:21-22).

This was our Lord's title at His birth and at His death, uttered by the Magi, the magistrates, the mob, and the markings over His cross. Jesus was and is the King of the Jews.

King of Israel

In a similar way, Jesus is named the King of Israel. The first person who called Him this title was a disciple named Nathanael. As described in John 1:49, he said to Jesus, "Rabbi, You are the Son of God! You are the King of Israel!"

Approximately three years later at the Lord's Triumphal Entry on Palm Sunday, large numbers of people celebrated His arrival in Jerusalem. And what did they say? "Hosanna! 'Blessed is He who comes in the name of the Lord!' The King of Israel!" (John 12:13)

Five days later as He suffered on Golgotha, one of His enemies shouted sarcastically, "If He is the King of Israel, let Him now come down from the cross, and we will believe Him" (Matthew 27:42).

As the King of Israel, Jesus is the ultimate fulfillment of the covenant God made with David. In 2 Samuel 7:12 and 16, the Lord said to David: "I will set up your seed after you, who will come from your body, and I will establish his kingdom.... And your house and your kingdom shall be established forever before you. Your throne shall be established forever."

According to this and other Scriptures, Jesus Christ is the only rightful everlasting heir to the throne of David. Isaiah 9:6-7 says: "For unto us a Child is born, unto us a Son is given; and the government will be upon His shoulder. And His name will be called Wonderful, Counselor, Mighty God, Everlasting Father, Prince of Peace. Of the increase of His government and peace there will be no end, upon the throne of David and over His kingdom, to order it and establish it with judgment and justice from that time forward, even forever. The zeal of the Lord of hosts will perform this."

Jesus is the rightful heir to the kingship of Israel because He comes through the lineage of David.

King of Kings

The Bible also calls Jesus the King of kings. This is our Lord's ultimate title of royal honor. In Revelation 19:11-16, the apostle John foresaw the Second Coming and said, "I saw heaven standing open and there before me was a white horse, whose rider is called Faithful and True. With justice he judges and wages war. His eyes are like blazing fire, and on his head are many crowns. He has a name written on him that no one knows but he himself. He is dressed in a robe dipped in blood, and his name is the Word of God. The armies of heaven were following him, riding on white horses and dressed in fine linen, white and clean. Coming out of his mouth is a sharp sword with which to strike down the nations. 'He will rule them with an iron scepter.' He treads the winepress of the fury of the wrath of God Almighty. On his robe and on his thigh he has this name written: KING OF KINGS AND LORD OF LORDS" (NIV).

When He returns, everyone will know who He is. It will be written on His clothing.

We live in a disturbed world. But none of today's politicians, leaders, or villains will ever gain supreme authority over Him, not even the coming Antichrist. All of them will falter and fail. Only Jesus is the King of kings and the Lord of lords.

We should be glad He's our Savior, our Shepherd, our Friend. But we should be especially glad He is Supreme Commander of the Universe and beyond—King of kings and Lord of lords.

King Over All the Earth

When He returns, Jesus will also be known as King Over All the Earth. In Zechariah 14, God says: "I will gather all the nations to Jerusalem to fight against it.... Then the Lord will go out and fight against those nations, as he fights on a day of battle. On that day his feet will stand on the Mount of Olives, east of Jerusalem, and the Mount of Olives will be split in two from east to west.... It will be a unique day—a day known only to the Lord.... On that day living water will flow out from Jerusalem, half of it east to the Dead Sea and half of it west to the Mediterranean Sea, in summer and in winter. The Lord will be king over the whole earth. On that day there will be one Lord, and his name the only name" (verses 2-9, NIV).

This raises a question about the timing of Christ's kingdom. In some biblical passages, it appears that the Kingdom of God is in the future, but other passages assume the Kingdom of God is now. The confusion clears up when we remember the sequence of the two comings of Christ. Jesus came the first time as a Redeeming King, and He is coming the second time as a Reigning King. He came the first time to establish a spiritual kingdom, His Church, to take the Gospel to the world. When He comes again, He will establish a political and a governmental kingdom to oversee the world for a thousand years.

The kingdom was inaugurated when He came the first time. It will be consummated when He comes again, and He will be King Over All the Earth.

King of Glory

When Jesus was in heaven before coming to earth, He was co-reigning with the Father and the Holy Spirit on the throne. One day the Father came to His Son and said something to this effect, "Son, we need to go take care of the sin problem, and there is only One who can do that and it's You."

We can almost hear Jesus saying, "Lord, God, My Father, I am willing."

So Jesus came down to earth for some thirty years and lived His life in perfection. Evil men nailed Him to a cross. He died and was buried, and He rose again. But after spending forty days with His disciples, the day came for Him to return to heaven. He didn't come here to stay. It was a round trip. On the same ridge to which He will soon return—the Mount of Olives—Jesus ascended into heaven.

Try to imagine what it was like in heaven when Jesus returned. The psalmist gives us an indication in Psalm 24:7-10: "Lift up your heads, O you gates! And be lifted up, you everlasting doors! And the King of glory shall come in. Who is this King of glory? The Lord strong and mighty, the Lord mighty in battle. Lift up your heads, O you gates! Lift up, you everlasting doors! And the King of glory shall come in. Who is this King of glory? The Lord of hosts, He is the King of glory."

Can you get a sense of the thrill and worship that arose from the angels around the throne? That's how we should worship our Lord today! He is the King of the Jews, King of Israel, King of kings, King Over All the Earth, and the King of glory!

His Regal Throne

Wouldn't you love to see how the throne of God looks in heaven right now? Wouldn't you love to see what Jesus is doing there? His throne is described to us in Isaiah 6, visualizing the scene as God describes it in His Word. The reality of this scene should always be in our mind.

Colossians 3:1-2 says, "If then you were raised with Christ, seek those things which are above, where Christ is, sitting at the right hand of God. Set your mind on things above, not on things on the earth."

When was the last time you meditated on the enthroned Christ seated at the right hand of the Father? His rule and reign means we should praise Him with all our heart, bring Him all our needs, trust Him in all our circumstances, and anticipate Him through all our days.

Praise Him With All Your Heart

First, we should praise Him with all of our heart. We should worship Him. Remember when the Magi bowed down and worshiped the Christ Child? They worshiped Him in His humility as the King of the Jews. How much more should we worship Him now as the King of kings in glory?

In Revelation 5, we have a vivid example of how the heavenly hosts render worship to Him who is on the throne: "And I looked, and behold, in the midst of the throne and of the four living creatures, and in the midst of the elders, stood a Lamb as though it had been slain, having seven horns and seven eyes, which are the seven Spirits of God sent out into all the earth. . . . And every creature which is in heaven and on the earth and under the earth and such as are in the sea, and all that are in them, I heard saying: 'Blessing and honor and glory and power be to Him who sits on the throne, and to the Lamb, forever and ever!'" (verses 6, 13)

You and I can join in the worship. We can start worshiping now. We can bless the One with honor and glory and power to Him who sits on the throne, the Lamb, forever and ever. We learn to praise like we learned how to pray. We just do it, over and over again until it becomes perfected in our lives. He is worthy of our praise, and it's our privilege and joy to lift up our voices to Him in adoration.

Bring Him All Your Needs

His throne is the ultimate destination of our prayers. In 2 Kings 19, we read of the time the Assyrian army encircled the city of Jerusalem. King Hezekiah had no hope of saving his throne or his people. The Assyrian emperor sent a letter demanding his surrender. But Hezekiah turned to another King, seeking deliverance. He went to the temple and spread out the letter before the Lord praying, "Lord, the God of Israel, enthroned between the cherubim, you alone are God over all the kingdoms of the earth. You have made heaven and earth" (verse 15, NIV). As he prayed to Him who sat on the throne, the Lord sent a mighty answer and the city was miraculously saved.

We can do the same with our perplexities and our problems. The example of Hezekiah is a visual picture of kneeling before the throne and spreading out our problems. We can take our burdens to the Lord and leave them there. Hebrews 4:16 says, "Let us therefore come boldly to the throne of grace, that we may obtain mercy and find grace to help in time of need."

We are actually praying to the One seated upon the throne of all the earth, and every good and perfect gift comes down from His heavenly throne.

Trust Him in All Your Circumstances

We can also trust Him in all our circumstances. One of the most-loved biblical promises speaks of God's providential control over our lives. Romans 8:28 says, "And we know that all things work together for good to those who love God, to those who are the called according to His purpose." One of the reasons God turns our burdens into blessings is because Jesus Christ is praying for us. Romans 8:34 says, "Who is he who condemns? It is Christ who died, and furthermore is also risen, who is even at the right hand of God, who also makes intercession for us."

Not until we get to heaven will we know what He has done for us beyond our knowledge, behind the scenes. Because Jesus is on His throne, we can press forward with endurance, knowing He is praying for us and watching over our circumstances. Someone once said, "We need to make sure we stay under everything that is above us, so that we can stay over everything that is below us." We need to remain surrendered to the sovereign control of Almighty God, leaving everything that crosses our path in His capable hands.

Anticipate Him Through All Your Days

Finally, we should anticipate the moment when we see the throne in the center of New Jerusalem. Revelation 22:1 says, "And he showed me a pure river of water of life, clear as crystal, proceeding from the throne of God and of the Lamb." Try to imagine the center of that glorious city, the spectacular throne of God. Jesus is sitting there at the headwaters of the crystal river that flows throughout the city. Oh, the anticipation that should bring to our heart. No wonder the end of the chapter includes these words: "Even so, come, Lord Jesus!" (Revelation 22:20)

Except for Christ, all leaders are flawed. Many have unleashed wars, triggered riots, annihilated opponents, bankrupted treasuries, and acted as fools. Others have exhibited great courage and demonstrated legendary leadership. But only Jesus Christ is King of the Jews, King of Israel, King of kings, King Over All the Earth, and the King of glory!

1. Read Psalm 95:1-3. We're told here to sing to the Lord and shout joyfully, to come before Him with thanksgiving and with psalms. According to verse 3, why should we do this?

2. Read Matthew 2:1-6 and list all the names and titles for Jesus in this passage.

3. Read Revelation 19:11-16. This is a depiction of the Second Coming of Christ. How many names and titles for Jesus are recorded in this passage?

4. Read Colossians 3:1-4.

   a. Where is Christ right now?

b. What are we commanded here to do?

c. In practical terms, what are some of the ways we can do this?

d. What are we promised in verse 4?

5. Read Revelation 19:11-16, making note again of the titles and names ascribed to Jesus.

a. How should this passage affect our worship now?

b. How can you take this attitude with you to church for your corporate worship experience?

6. Read 2 Kings 19:14-19.

    a. Have you ever had an experience that in some way resembles what Hezekiah did here? If so, describe what occurred.

    b. How can we better understand the power of our Lord's throne?

7. Read Hebrews 4:16.

    a. Do you think this verse is a good description of Hezekiah's actions in 2 Kings 19?

    b. Why is this throne called a "throne of grace"?

GROUP QUESTIONS

1. Has anyone in your group visited a castle or toured anything associated with royalty? What would be the joys and burdens of being a monarch today? Would you like to belong to a royal family?

2. As Christians, we do belong to a royal family, for our Savior, Jesus, is a multi-faceted King. As a group, review His royal names from this lesson and isolate the one that is most encouraging to each of you and discuss why that is true.

3. According to this lesson, there are four implications of the kingship of Jesus. First, we should praise Him with all our heart. Read Revelation 5:8-14.

   a. What elements of worship can you isolate in this passage?

   b. What can we learn from this passage about corporate worship?

4. Second, we should bring Him all our needs. Compare 2 Kings 19:14-19 with Hebrews 4:16. Exactly how do we do that today? Has anyone in your group ever had an experience like this?

5. We should also trust Him with all our circumstances. Read Psalm 11:1-4. Why was David able to reject the urge to flee like a bird to a distant mountain?

6. Lastly, we should live in anticipation of Him throughout our life here on earth. Read Revelation 22:1-5. It is a vivid description of the center of the eternal city of New Jerusalem. Discuss what you are most eager to see in the eternal city.

DID YOU KNOW?

On the most important occasions of state, Queen Elizabeth II wears the Imperial State Crown, which is adorned with nearly three thousand precious stones, including the Cullinan II diamond, St. Edward's Sapphire, the Stuart Sapphire, and the Black Prince's Ruby. During the reign of Queen Victoria, the crown suffered an accident as it was being carried by the Duke of Argyll at the State Opening of Parliament in 1845. It fell off its cushion and broke. Queen Victoria later wrote, "It was all crushed and squashed like a pudding." The gems were remounted and in 1953, the size was adjusted for the coronation of Queen Elizabeth II.

ADDITIONAL RESOURCES
by Dr. David Jeremiah

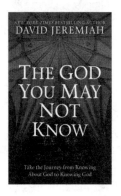

The God You May Not Know

Some say the greatest question in life is: "Does God exist?" But Dr. Jeremiah asks, "Do we know the God who *does* exist?" The study of God is the supreme study of a lifetime—it lifts our thoughts, steadies our nerves, and expands our confidence. In this companion book to *The Jesus You May Not Know*, learn how to develop an intimacy with God you may never have known before as you discover *The God You May Not Know*.

Revealing the Mysteries of Heaven

What happens when we die? Where do we go? Is there an afterlife? Does the Bible say anything specific about heaven? *Revealing the Mysteries of Heaven* closes the gap between what the Bible says about heaven and what the average believer knows. By studying the Scriptures from Genesis to Revelation the curtain is pulled back—to the extent Scripture allows—to reveal the glorious and utterly amazing realm of heaven.

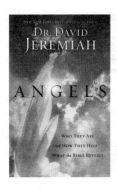

Angels

People have long been fascinated by stories of angel sightings, yet many contemporary beliefs about angels are based on misconception and myth. In *Angels*, Dr. David Jeremiah uses Scripture to unveil the remarkable truth about these agents of heaven and their role and work in our world. This book will capture the attention of readers of all ages who seek a broad and thorough survey of Scripture that clearly separates fact from fiction as it relates to angels.

Understanding the 66 Books of the Bible

Understanding the 66 Books of the Bible is a resource to orient you to the who, what, when, and where of each book in the Bible. Whether you're a new reader or a veteran student, whether you want to visit the Gospel of John or take a journey into Nahum or Jude—this is the guide for you. In this resource you will find a summary for each book, along with a key thought, key verse, key action, and prayer. It will be the fastest journey through the Bible you will ever experience!

Each of these resources was created from a teaching series by Dr. David Jeremiah. Contact Turning Point for more information about correlating materials.

For pricing information and ordering, contact us at

P.O. Box 3838
San Diego, CA 92163
(800) 947-1993
www.DavidJeremiah.org

STAY CONNECTED
to Dr. David Jeremiah

Take advantage of three great ways to let Dr. David Jeremiah give you spiritual direction every day!

Turning Points Magazine and Devotional

Receive Dr. David Jeremiah's magazine, *Turning Points*, each month:

- Thematic study focus
- 52 pages of life-changing reading
- Relevant articles
- Special features
- Daily devotional readings
- Bible study resource offers
- Live event schedule
- Radio & television information

Request *Turning Points* magazine today!
(800) 947-1993 | DavidJeremiah.org/Magazine

Daily Turning Point E-Devotional

Start your day off right! Find words of inspiration and spiritual motivation waiting for you on your computer every morning! Receive a daily e-devotion communication from David Jeremiah that will strengthen your walk with God and encourage you to live the authentic Christian life.

Sign up for your free e-devotional today!
www.DavidJeremiah.org/Devo

Turning Point Mobile App

Access Dr. David Jeremiah's video teachings, audio sermons, and more... whenever and wherever you are!

Download your free app today!
www.DavidJeremiah.org/App